PENGUIN BOOKS
MAHAYANA TANTRA

Shri Dharmakirti, a disciple of His Holiness the Fourteenth Dalai
Lama, was born in a Sikh family at Shimla, in the Himalayan
mountains. He studied biochemistry in college, and later worked
as an advertising executive and computer programmer. After
encountering the Prasangika Madhyamika system of Arya
Nagarjuna, he 'left home' when he was twenty-seven, and became
a disciple of His Holiness the Dalai Lama. During the six years he
spent at the feet of his Guru in Dharamsala, he received the initiations
and further instructions in the practice of Highest Secret Mantra,
and was inducted into the lineage of Lama Tsongkhapa. He now
lives in retreat in the Kullu valley, and occasionally teaches.

The author can be contacted on: tathagata_garbha@yahoo.co.in

Shri Dharmakirti

Mahayana Tantra

An Introduction

PENGUIN BOOKS

An imprint of Penguin Random House

PENGUIN BOOKS

USA | Canada | UK | Ireland | Australia
New Zealand | India | South Africa | China | Singapore

Penguin Books is part of the Penguin Random House group of companies
whose addresses can be found at global.penguinrandomhouse.com

Published by Penguin Random House India Pvt. Ltd
4th Floor, Capital Tower 1, MG Road,
Gurugram 122 002, Haryana, India

Penguin
Random House
India

First published by Penguin Books India 2002

Copyright © Shri Dharmakirti 2002

All rights reserved

10 9 8 7 6 5 4 3 2

ISBN 9780143028536

Typeset in Sabon by Mantra Virtual Services, New Delhi
Printed at Repro India Limited

www.penguin.co.in

MIX
Paper from
responsible sources
FSC® C047271

This is a legitimate digitally printed version of the book and therefore might not
have certain extra finishing on the cover.

To the long life and continued presence of His Holiness the Dalai Lama. And to the memory of Madhusudan Singh, who first taught me about cyclic existence and emptiness.

Contents

Introduction   ix

Tantric History   1
The Tantric Practitioner   17
Tantric World View   57
The Tantric Guru   77
The Tantric Path   104
Conclusion   155

Appendix-I   159
Appendix-II   162
Notes   167
Glossary   172

Arya Manjushree

Introduction

'*The greatest profundities can be found in Highest Yoga Tantra.*'
—His Holiness The Dalai Lama

Namas Swaraswatyai cha guru Manju ghoshaya cha.
(Homage to Swaraswati and guru Manju Ghosh.)[1]

THE PRACTITIONER OF Mahayana Buddhist Tantra is a marvellous being—a spiritual warrior par excellence. Unbidden, such a person takes on the responsibility of delivering all sentient beings from *samsara*, the recurrent cycle of birth-death and rebirth. In order to accomplish this task, the Tantric Bodhisattva[2] dons the armour of moral discipline and patience and acquires the laser sharp intellectual sword of Madhyamic reasoning that penetrates to the heart of reality. He carries with him the impenetrable shield of universal compassion. Riding on the two-winged white steed of Bodhichitta,[3] such a one proceeds to seek out and decapitate the two greatest enemies of those aspiring to the spiritual path—'self-grasping' and 'self-cherishing'.

Avoiding the abyss of the two extremes of *samsara* and Nirvana, moving swiftly along the wide highway of the Mahayana, empowered by the Vajradhara guru,[4] such a practitioner fearlessly delves into the deepest recesses of the mind in order to find the ultimate wish-fulfilling gem of Clear Light which is guarded by Yama, the lord of death. Defeating and subduing Yama, the Tantric Bodhisattva uses that gem to attain the highest possible state of existence— Buddhahood—a union of omniscient mind and immortal form. He then proceeds to work ceaselessly, in countless bodies, to deliver all sentient beings over the endless continuum of their lives, stretching over vast periods of time.

This is not an allegory or a myth but a realistic undertaking. An example of this was Buddha himself who started out as an un-omniscient mortal like the rest of us. Having achieved Enlightenment, he taught others how to achieve this state. Since then, many hundreds of thousands of human beings, who have had the good karma to encounter this system, have traversed this path and reached their goal. Many are still in the process of accomplishing it. Due to the ceaseless efforts of great gurus like His Holiness the Dalai Lama, many others will, in future, practise this system and accomplish their goal. His Holiness has repeatedly demonstrated the efficacy of this path by deliberately incarnating fourteen times since the First Dalai Lama, Gyalwa Gendun Drub, appeared in the fourteenth century in Tibet. For the past 600 years, incarnations of the Dalai Lamas (and other Tibetan gurus) have guided thousands of fortunate beings like myself over the continuum of our lives, starting afresh in each life where we left off in the previous one, having been stopped by Yamaraja.

In my case, the propensity to follow this path, the seeds of which were sown in many former lives, was activated when I first beheld the Guru in a public meeting at Gangtok,

Sikkim, when I was twenty-two years old. The subsequent turn of events made me contemplate death and the impermanence of life which awakened within me the seeds of renunciation. Subsequently, I made great effort to seek out the profound Buddhist doctrine of Emptiness after being exhorted to do so by my father, Madhusudan Singh, on the point of his death. Having sought and found a definitive translation of a Prasangika Madhyamika text as it is studied and practised by the Geluk-pa order of Tibetan Buddhism,[5] in the winter of 1987, at the age of twenty-seven, I 'left home' and found my way back to the lotus feet of my Guru.

His Holiness supported me for six years while I stayed at Dharamsala, first in the Buddhist School of Dialectics, then in solitary retreat in the forest above Mcleodganj, and, eventually, in a small cottage near His Holiness's residence at Thekchencholing. During this period, I completed the '1,00,000 preliminaries', and received from His Holiness the empowerments of Highest Yoga Tantra[6] along with further instructions on the practice of meditation. I also received detailed teachings on the 'Lam-Rim'[7] from the Very Venerable Lati Rimpochay, a former abbot of Ganden Shartse Monastery.

I remember, at one point, after having received the empowerment of Vajrabhairava, I presented a painting I had made of the deity for meditative visualization to His Holiness. After examining it with some delight, he pointed to the mantra of the deity which I had written in Sanskrit at the bottom of the painting. After making me recite it, he asked me why I had written the syllables 'HUNG HUNG' in Tibetan at the end of the mantra, while the rest of the mantra was in Sanskrit. I replied that I thought that the syllable 'HUNG' was of Tibetan derivation! He told me emphatically, 'All of this has come from India, none of this is a Tibetan invention.' His answer struck me like a thunderbolt; it was as if he had bequeathed to me the core of my Indian identity. That this awesome body of knowledge and practice—compared to which the entire corpus of scientific knowledge is as basic as children playing with marbles—was a creation of Indian minds is something that never fails to amaze me even today.

So this book is not only an account of my exploration into the 'body of Reality' but also, in an immediate and intimate sense, an exploration into the heart of Mother India.

Today, quite a few modern educated Indians regard the mere mention of the word 'Tantra' with suspicion and apprehension. For them Tantra evokes images of shady sadhus and yogis stalking the corridors of power in Delhi and of fake godmen, conning the gullible with mumbo-jumbo. They associate Tantra with weird rituals to bloodthirsty goddesses and gods, animal and human sacrifice and with black magic. Buddhist Tantra, which has been absent from the Indian mainstream for over a thousand years, is far removed from such shamanism. Perhaps what goes by the name of Tantra today is the degenerated version of an 'original' Buddhist Tantric culture that flourished prior to the eighth century in various regions spanning from Khotan and Bamiyan to Kashmir and the Swat valley (in Pakistan); from Dhaka and Angkor to Andhra Pradesh. All these regions were devastated by the sword of Islam. The only region that escaped unscathed was Tibet. And it was in Tibet that renowned Indian Buddhist gurus began transplanting the crucial lineages of Tantra, starting in the eighth century with the great guru Padmasambhava who travelled from India to Tibet, to the eleventh century when

Dipankara Shri Gyan Atisha, who was also known as the last great 'Lion of Dharma', went to Tibet, worked and died there. It is my belief that many Indian practitioners and disciples of these gurus followed their masters to Tibet—after dying in India and being reborn in Tibet, as Tibetans.

Thus, today, Tibet is the sole repository of the original Tantric tradition in its complete, untainted form. Tibetan culture and society have carefully preserved and transmitted this precious tradition from generation to generation. We are fortunate that despite the Chinese Communist invasion of Tibet in 1949, and their subsequent systematic attempts to wipe out Tibetan Buddhism, all the crucial lineages of Maha Anuttara Yoga Tantra have survived in treasure houses like His Holiness the Dalai Lama and the other patriarchs and yogis who constitute the Tibetan diaspora.

I write with the hope and the intention that through this book many others, specially Indians, be inspired to seek out, learn, and thereby preserve this tradition for the coming generations. That is, for ourselves and our future incarnations.

🔲

1. Tantric History

'I am the teacher,
I am the teaching,
as the listener, I am even the assembly.'
                                    —Hevajra Tantra

AFTER MANIFESTING COMPLETE Enlightenment under the Bodhi tree at Magadha, Buddha Shakyamuni Gautam Siddhartha 'turned the wheel of Dharma' (Sanskrit: *Dharma-chakra-pravartan*), by teaching various assemblies of disciples how to reach such a state.

To beginners, the Buddha taught the path of renunciation, or the Hinayana, where the emphasis is on completely renouncing the passions and seeking a personal Nirvana, which means an end to the cycle of uncontrolled birth-death and rebirth. Such a path has been the ideal of the renunciant monk (or nun)—the Bhikshu (or Bhikshuni)—and was exemplified by such disciples as Shariputra, Mahamaudgalyana, Mahakashyap and others. Since this is the most accessible level, it spread widely, and survives till today in Sri Lanka, Thailand and Burma, where it is considered to be the only path that the Buddha taught.

To more advanced assemblies of disciples, i.e. those who were well established on the path of renunciation of *samsara* (cyclic existence), the Buddha taught the Mahayana and the ideal of the Bodhisattva, which emphasized 'great compassion' for others.

The Bodhisattva, the spiritual warrior, did not seek a hasty exit from *samsara* through a personal Nirvana, but selflessly worked in *samsara* for the benefit of others. The Bodhisattva did this for 'Three Mahakalpas' (great aeons of time), accumulating the 'provisions' of merit (*punya*) and wisdom (*pragya*), and thereby ascending the ten Bodhisattva levels of inner evolution towards complete Buddhahood— a state far higher than that of personal Nirvana. This level of the Buddha's teaching was more restricted as it involved the use of the passions for the sake of others, much as a wise parent would use the 'devices' of love and anger for the benefit of a child. The teaching being restricted, did not spread openly, and was exemplified by such Bodhisattvas as the 'four close sons'—Manjushree, Avalokiteshwara, Vajrapani and Maitreya—monks such as Subhuti and Mahamati, laymen like the Lichchavi Vimalakirti, and laywomen like the queen Srimala Devi. After the passing away of the Buddha, the texts of this cycle of teaching—the *Pragyaparamita Sutras*—were entrusted to the care of the Nagas for posterity, but were retrieved from them by Nagarjuna, promulgator of Mahayana, whose coming had been prophesied earlier by the Buddha in the Lankavatara Sutra.

The Vajrayana[1], or the Tantric path, was taught by the Buddha to assemblies of those great Bodhisattva yogis who were well established on the path towards renunciation and Great Compassion. They had attained sufficient purity of mind to be able to 'metabolize' the poisons of lust and anger, and to transform the energy of the passions into the wisdom of the non-duality of subject and object. Due to the purity of their minds, they were able to perceive the Buddha's subtle form—the Sambhogakaya—and to receive teachings directly from it.

Thus, on the fifteenth day of the third month, a year after his Enlightenment, while teaching the *Pragyaparamita Sutras* on Vulture Peak at Magadha in the ordinary form of a monk, the Buddha simultaneously appeared in the subtle form of Buddha Kalachakra to King Suchandra of Shambhala at Dhanyakataka in south India (Amrawati, Guntoor district, Andhra Pradesh). He taught the king the cycle of teachings that were compiled by him as the *Kalachakra Tantra*. Similarly, the Buddha appeared in the subtle Sambhogakaya form of Buddha Guhyasamaja to King Indrabhuti of Oddiyana (Swat valley), and gave him the cycle of Tantric teachings which were compiled by the king and came to be known as the *Guhyasamaja Tantra*.

KING INDRABODHI AND THE EIGHTY-FOUR MAHASIDDHAS OF INDIA[2]

The *Guhyasamaja Tantra* is considered to be the king of all Tantras, for the Buddha has said that if the *Guhyasamaja* exists, the complete path to Enlightenment exists. Its importance also stems from the fact that most of the later Tantras were derived from it. Just as the *Guhyasamaja* is the king of Tantras, King Indrabodhi (Indrabhuti) is considered to be the progenitor of most of the Tantric lineages that developed in India and Tibet. Tantric lore says that he practised the *Guhyasamaja Tantra* without renouncing the pleasures and comforts of a king, and so skilful was he that he was able to lead his entire retinue, and the inhabitants of his capital, on the path of the *Guhyasamaja* till all of them attained the Rainbow Body[3] and vanished in a blaze of light.

The city became desolate and was eventually covered by a lake, in the centre of which the Tantric texts compiled by King Indrabodhi were preserved on an island, guarded by a class of supernatural yoginis called Dakinis. This island became known as the 'Gagan ganj' library, and many subsequent masters collectively known as the Eighty-Four Mahasiddhas, were guided to this library by visions and dreams, and retrieved from it specific Tantras meant for certain types of disciples, at specific times. It is said that the library still exists but is not meant for the uninitiated.

The lineage of the *Guhyasamaja Tantra*, and other Tantras derived from it, was transmitted through King Indrabodhi to such Mahasiddhas as Kuttaraja (Lord of Bitches), the princess Goma Devi, the Brahmin Saraha, and others. In the first century A.D., the famous Arya Nagarjuna received, compiled and extensively commented on the *Guhyasamaja* and other major Tantras, thus starting the Tantric cycle of teachings known as the Arya Cycle.

THE GLORIOUS NAGARJUNA

Nagarjuna, protector of Dharma, is second in importance to the Buddha. Called the 'Second Buddha', he extensively upheld, protected and propagated the lineages of the Mahayana and Vajrayana. He is said to have lived for 600 years by mastering the science of alchemy. Through his expertise in sorcery, he subdued the 'Mother Goddesses'

(Matarah) of the Indian subcontinent and is said to have had a retinue of Yakshinis.[4] He spent many years in the realm of the Nagas and retrieved from them the *Pragyaparamita Sutras* and various texts such as the Tantras of Tara and Mahakala.

Writing the definitive commentary on the *Guhyasamaja*, called the *Five Stages* (Panchakram), Nagarjuna transmitted the system to close disciples like Aryadeva, Nagabodhi and Chandrakirti. Chandrakirti's commentary, called *Clarifying Lamp*, on Nagarjuna's *Five Stages* forms the backbone of the practice of Tantra in Tibet.

By the sixth century A.D., the Mahayana Tantric tradition had reached its pinnacle in India. Many major Tantric cycles had appeared and spread widely, from central Asia to Indonesia. By now, the Tantras were classified into two main categories of Father Tantras and Mother Tantras. The former dwelt on the yogas of the 'Illusory Body' that resulted in the attainment of the Rupakaya (form body) of a Buddha, while the latter concentrated on generating the 'Ground State' of Clear Light through the focused use of bliss. The Father Tantras comprise the *Guhyasamaja*, *Vajrabhairava* and *Yamari* cycles, and the Mother Tantras comprise the *Heruka Chakrasamvara*, *Hevajra* and *Vajra yogini* cycles. Each Tantra comprised a root-text that contained a complete set of instructions on meditative techniques that were capable of bringing enlightenment to a particular type of trainee. The Mahasiddha adepts secretly propagated these Tantra cycles in hermitages from generation to generation. Great masters like Jalandharipada, Krishnacharya, Dombi Heruka, Luipada and Vajraghantapada emerged from these lineages.

By the eighth century A.D., barbarians had begun to

overrun the Tantric world, starting in West Asia. In Khotan, Kashmir and Swat valley, monasteries were ransacked, monks were killed, and centuries-old texts were burnt. As the danger approached closer to the Buddhist heartland of India, it became imperative to find a safe haven for the Tantric tradition.

To accomplish this, the Bodhisattva Manjushri incarnated as the King of Tibet, Trhisong Detsen (eighth century A.D.), and the Bodhisattva Arya Avalokiteshwara incarnated in India as the Awesome Tantric Master Padmasambhava. It is said that he was not born from a human womb but spontaneously arose as an eight-year-old boy from the centre of a giant lotus in a lake at Oddiyana.

THE TRANSMISSION OF THE TANTRIC TRADITION TO TIBET

The royal family of Tibet had begun to come under the influence of Buddhism as early as the fifth century A.D. By the 8th century A.D., the young crown prince, Trhisong Detsen, was brought up as a Buddhist and after assuming power as king, decided to proclaim Buddhism as the state religion. He decided to establish the first monastic centre in Tibet along the lines of the great Indian monastic centres at Nalanda, Taxila, Vikramsila and Odantapuri. In order to accomplish this, he invited the great Indian Preceptor, the Venerable Bhikshu Shantarakshita, to come to Tibet and lay the foundation of the first monastic centre at Samyeling, near the capital Lhasa. He also ordered seven of the brightest young men from seven of the foremost Tibetan noble families to be ordained as novice monks under the Venerable

Preceptor. These seven became the first members of the monastic Sangha in Tibet and became known as the 'seven who were Tested'.

The Venerable Preceptor Shantarakshita found himself unable to establish the monastery at Samyeling, because whatever construction work was completed during the day, was undone at night by malevolent forces under the control of the native Bon Shamanistic priests. The Venerable Preceptor, being a Bhikshu, was restrained by his vows from combating the evil forces and therefore requested the king to invite the Tantric master Padmasambhava to come and subdue them.

On coming to Tibet, Padmasambhava was venerated by the king and his retinue as their prime guru. The king begged him to bring the complete teachings of the Buddha into Tibet, and as guru dakshina (offering to the guru), offered him everything, including himself, his country, his consorts, and possessions.

After initiating the king and his close retinue of twenty-five into the Highest Tantras, Padmasambhava proceeded to bring the entire teachings pertaining to Dharma into Tibet. Under his guidance, Buddhist scholars were invited from India to train translators. Many young men were ordained as monks, and the essentials of Sutra and Tantra were translated from Sanskrit into Tibetan. Padmasambhava subdued the malevolent spirits, gods and goddesses of Tibet and bound them under oath to protect and preserve the Dharma. He supervised the construction of Samyeling and patterned it on the model of the Odantapuri Vihar. It is said that Padmasambhava, in the company of his consort, the Tibetan princess Kharchen-dza, Yeshe Tso-gyal, covered the whole of Tibet by foot, concealing texts and other

Dharma-treasures called 'Termas' (Dharma texts and ritual objects) in many secret places, which were found later by prophesied gurus and were propagated by them.

During Padmasambhava's stay in Tibet, many Tantric experts there attained the highest realization, and the cycle of translation, study, practise and propagation of the Sutras and Tantras of Buddhism began. The lineages of Tantra, such as the extremely esoteric Dzokchen Atiyoga that were established by Padmasambhava, are still alive and are propagated by the oldest of the four major Tibetan Buddhist orders—the Nyingma-pa.

After single-handedly ensuring that the best minds in Tibet became well-versed in the Highest Tantric Dharma and the study and practice of the core of Indian Dharma began to be passed on from generation to generation, legend has it that Padmasambhava rode off into the sky from the peak of Kungtang mountain—'his robes fluttering and the rings of his trident staff jingling'. He is said to be still alive in the form of Kapala Mala (Tibetan: *Thothreng-tsal*)—the 'skull-garlanded' king of rakshasas—on the mystical island of Camradvipa, in the ocean south-west of the Indian subcontinent.

Thereafter, although the monastic tradition declined due to persecution by the apostate king, Lang Darma, the tradition of Secret Mantra was maintained unbroken by white-robed householder yogis residing in remote hermitages. By the ninth century, the ancient royal Yarlung dynasty of kings died out; Tibet disintegrated into several warring kingdoms, and the public practice of Dharma declined.

Meanwhile, the Indian heartland was being ravaged and overrun by barbarians from the west and the great monastic centres of learning were being ransacked and destroyed. As the cycle of study and learning at the monastic centres was disrupted, the flow of Dharma from generation to generation too was interrupted. The sun of Dharma began to set over India. And then as if in a last brilliant flash, the great gurus, the Mahasiddhas Tilopa, Naropa, and the Mahapandita Dipankara Shri Gyan Atisha, appeared in the late tenth century A.D.

In Tibet, after a brief decline following the end of the ancient dynasty of kings, Dharma underwent a revival as local kings patronized scholars and translators who risked life and limb to travel to India to re-learn the Dharma and to invite the last of the great Indian gurus to Tibet. The translator Marpa-choe-ki-lodoe travelled to India and Nepal to learn the Tantras at the feet of Mahasiddha Naropa and 108 other Indian gurus. From them he received transmissions of the *Guhyasamaja*, *Hevajra*, *Heruka* and many other Tantras. He also received from his principal guru, Naropa, the unique lineage of the *Six Yogas of Naropa* which condensed essential practices from both Mother and Father Tantras into a unified whole. On returning to Tibet, he founded the prolific Kagyu order, which multiplied into many sub-sects, and produced great yogis like Mila-Repa. The Kagyu-pa order flourishes today under the care of patriarchs like the Gyalwa Karmapa Lama. The translator Drok-mi lotsawa learned the *Hevajra Tantra* at the feet of the Master Gayadhara and founded the Sakyapa order that flourishes today under the Sakya patriarchs.

The last of the great masters to travel from India to Tibet was Dipankara Shri Gyan Atisha. He founded the

Kadampa order in which he reunified the tradition of Sutra and Tantra which had grown apart and seemed to many people to be contradictory and irreconcilable. In his seminal text *Bodhipatha Pradipa* (Lamp on the Path to Enlightenment), Atisha re-established the Sutrayana as the ethical and philosophical basis of the Tantric path, showing a stepwise continuity from the Sutras to the Tantras. His followers, the famous Kadampa Geshes, re-established strict monasticism as the basis of the Vajrayana, and it was from them that the lineage of the Dalai Lamas eventually arose.

THE HOLY LINEAGE OF THE DALAI LAMAS

By the twelfth century A.D., Dharma was again flourishing in Tibet. The four major orders of Tibetan Buddhism had evolved their own unique identities which survive till today. The first lineage of incarnate lamas (gurus) had been established by the first Karmapa Lama—a lineal descendant of the Indian Mahasiddhas Tilopa and Naropa.

In the late fourteenth century, the prolific reformer Lama Tsongkhapa appeared. Having encountered the Bodhisattva Manjushree in the course of his visions, he received from him the Sutra and Tantra traditions of Nagarjuna and Chandrakirti. Reforming the Kadampa order established by Atisha, he unified the major Tantric traditions existent in Tibet, founded monastic centres of learning at Ganden, Drepung and Sera, and wrote extensive commentaries on the Sutras and Tantras. He established the practice of the four major Tantric cycles of Kalachakra, Guhyasamaja, Chakrasamvara and Vajrabhairava as the core Tantric practice of the Geluk-pa order in the fifteenth century A.D., basing it on strict monasticism. He constructed the three-dimensional mandalas of Guhyasamaja, Chakrasamvara and Vajrabhairava in minute detail at his hermitage at Ganden. His teachings spread widely and one of his disciples, the future Dalai Lama, later established his teachings as the dominant Tibetan order.

One of Lama Tsongkhapa's foremost disciples, Gyalwa Gendun Drup, attained the highest siddhis through practising the Tantras. He demonstrated complete control over the process of death, intermediate state, and rebirth, by deliberately reincarnating in order to firmly establish his guru's teachings in Tibet. His incarnation was found when robbers attacked a nomadic encampment; the nomads fled, leaving behind a baby. On returning the next day, they were amazed to see the child playing safely under the shadow of a menacing raven that was protecting it from predators. The child was able to recall his former life and was recognized as the incarnation of Gyalwa Gendun Drup. Thus began the holy lineage of the Dalai Lamas, with the next incarnation, Gyalwa Sonam Gyatso, being given the title 'Dalai' (ocean) Lama by the Mongol ruler, Altan Khan, who revered him as his prime guru. The cordial relations between the Mongols and the Dalai Lamas saved Tibet from Mongol domination and depradations and consolidated the power of the Dalai Lamas.

In the seventeenth century, the fifth Dalai Lama, Gyalwa Lozang Gyatso, known as the 'Great Fifth', used the forces of the Mongol king, Ghushri Khan, to reunify Tibet. He built the vast Potala Palace at Lhasa as the symbol of Tibetan sovereignty and as the seat of spiritual and temporal authority that were unified in the person of the Dalai Lama. This unification became possible because by the seventeenth century, Tibet had evolved to the point where the prime purpose of the nation (i.e. politics and the national economy) was to nurture young men and women in vast monastic universities, nunneries and hermitages in order to produce Siddhas and Buddhas! The preservation and propagation of the Buddha-Dharma and the precious lineages of Secret Mantra became the focal point of Tibetan culture. By now, not only had the Tibetans translated the entire corpus of Mahayana and Vajrayana from Sanskrit to Tibetan but, through the practice of these teachings, Tibetan Masters were also able to teach directly from their own experience.

The Dalai Lama thus came to combine in his person the three separate functions of king, preceptor, and Tantric adept. It was a feat unmatched in human history. The Dalai Lama[5] appeared in each generation in a new body, in 'democratic' incarnations—sometimes in the household of a Tantric adept, at times in noble or royal families, and at other times in peasant and nomad households. And in each generation, he is the repository of the most precious Tantric lineages, transmitting them to generations of yogis and yoginis.

TANTRA TODAY

Thus, despite the barbaric invasions that completely destroyed Buddhism in India and the invasion of Tibet by Communist China, all the major Tantric lineages from ancient India are still alive and flourishing—thanks to the Tibetans. Today, Tibetan Buddhism exists in the form of four major orders—the Nyingma-pa, the Kagyu-pa, the Sakyapa and the Geluk-pa. These are the sole inheritors of the ancient Indian Buddhist Tantric culture. Whereas the Hinayana and Mahayana traditions of Buddhism spread to the south and north of the Indian subcontinent, the Vajrayana in its complete form spread only to Tibet.

Thus, these four Tibetan orders contain, in the persons of their gurus, in their scriptures and texts, and in their living cycles of ritual, art and practice, the entire set of instructions known as Highest Yoga Tantra (Maha-anuttara-Yoga-Tantra) that lead to the attainment of the Trikaya (Three Bodies) of a fully Enlightened Buddha. These teachings do not exist outside these four Tibetan orders.

THE NYINGMA-PA

The Nyingma-pa are followers of Padmasambhava and his lineal descendants. In their scriptures, they follow the cycle of 'Old Translations' of the Tantras made prior to the time of Rinchen Zangpo (954–1055 A.D.), whose translations of the Tantras form the scriptural basis of the three other Tibetan orders. The Nyingma-pa divide the practice of Highest Yoga Tantra into three phases called Maha-yoga, Anuyoga and Atiyoga (Dzokchen). The former two are preparatory to Atiyoga, in which a suitable disciple is directly introduced to the subtlest state of mind—equivalent to experiencing the deepest level of consciousness, which all ordinary beings unwittingly experience only at death. This is an advanced technique applicable only to highly evolved yogis who can sustain the impact of such a revelation without actually dying. Such a yogi could vanish in a flash of light, leaving no trace behind, and then reappear in one's old body (or any body) at will. An average yogi would vanish, leaving behind only hair, teeth and nails.

Known for their formidable magical abilities, the gurus and Tantric experts of this tradition practise and propagate their knowledge at hermitages and monasteries in Nepal, Sikkim, Bhutan and even in Chinese-occupied Tibet. They have no traditional patriarch, there being several hierarchs of different lineages within the Nyingma tradition. Two of the seniormost hierarchs—His Holiness Dudjom Rimpoche and His Holiness Dilgo Khyentse Rimpoche—passed away recently, their incarnations have been found and are now in their infancy. The Nyingma-pa have major centres in India in Dehradun, Himachal Pradesh and Karnataka.

THE KAGYU-PA

The Kagyu-pa are descendants of the Indian Mahasiddhas Tilopada, Maitripada, Naropada and their Tibetan disciple, the translator, Marpa Choe-ki-lodoe. They have various sub-sects, one of which—the Drukpa Kagyu—is the dominant Buddhist order in Bhutan. The largest of the sub-sects, the Karma-Kagyu, are followers of the Karmapa lamas who are the oldest incarnating lineage existing today, their seat-in-exile being at Rumtek in Sikkim. The present seventeenth Karmapa Lama, His Holiness Ugyen Thinley Dorje, was much in the news after his dramatic escape from Chinese-occupied Tibet to India. The Kagyu-pa principally practise and propagate various lineages of the Six Yogas of Naropa that combine the essential practices of the Father and Mother classes of Tantra. They are renowned for using the yogas of Inner-Heat (Tibetan: *Tummo*; Sanskrit: *Chandali*) and 'Consciousness-Transference' as the principal means of experiencing the state of 'Maha Mudra' (Great Seal) i.e., the Ultimate Reality. They have major centres in Sikkim, Nepal, Bhutan, Himachal Pradesh and Dehradun.

THE SAKYAPA

The Sakyapa are descendants of the Indian Mahasiddhas Virupa and Gayadhara, their practice is based on the *Hevajra Tantra*—one of the principal Mother Tantras. Their 'Lam-De' (path-result) practice combines the Sutras and Tantras, and followers of the order are noted for their scholarship. The present Sakya hierarch, His Holiness Sakya Tri-zin, has his seat at Dehradun.

THE GELUK-PA

The Geluk-pa are followers of Lama Tsongkhapa and the lineage of the Dalai Lamas. Laying stress on strict monasticism, the Geluk-pa are well-known for their dialectical prowess and analytical skill. They follow the 'Lam-Rim' (structured path) approach, laying great emphasis on a detailed study of the Sutras and Tantras before a trainee is allowed to practise Tantric meditation, thus upholding the ideal of the 'Scholar-Yogi'. In philosophy, they follow the Prasangika Madhyamika system of Arya Nagarjuna and Chandrakirti. In the practice of Tantra, they mainly follow the three cycles of Vajrabhairava as protector, Sri Heruka Chakrasamvara as the preliminary Clear-Light practice, and Guhyasamaja as the main illusory-body practice. They also follow the lineage of the Six Yogas of Naropa. The Dalai Lamas are renowned masters of the Kalachakra Tantra. They uphold many of the Nyingma-pa lineages such as the Vajra-Kilaya. After the destruction of the three great Geluk-pa monastic universities of Sera, Drepung and Ganden by the Chinese Communists, these centres have been re-established in exile in Karnataka, where the cycles of study and practice of the Sutras and Tantras are kept alive under the care of His Holiness the Dalai Lama.

Thus, for any serious seeker today, who wishes to learn and practise the path of Highest Yoga Tantra, it would be mandatory to follow one (or more) of these four orders. It would be essential to be guided in the preliminaries of Sutra and Tantra by a teacher. It would then be necessary to enter into a Guru-disciple relationship with one (or more) of the lineage-holding lamas (gurus) of these sects, from whom one would have to receive the complete set of initiations into one or more of the standard Mandalas of Highest Yoga Tantra.

One would then have to receive the so-called 'further-instruction' in the practice of the 'Generation and Completion' stages of Secret Mantra. It would then be necessary to find conditions of solitude and silence which are conducive to devoting one's entire energy to the practise of these paths. As His Holiness the Dalai Lama often says, it is necessary to start with the intention of spending not just a few months or a few years but one's entire life, and many future lives, in the pursuit of the path to Enlightenment. Only then might it be possible to attain Complete Enlightenment in this life.

▣

2. The Tantric Practitioner

*'How Can Someone Who Cherishes Self
more than others
Take Lust and Such Dangerous Poisons
for food?'*

—Dharmarakshita (tenth century A.D.)
The Wheel of Sharp Weapons

THE BUDDHIST WORLD view regards the present times as the 'dark age' (Kali Yuga), rife with the five degenerations. These are: 1. The degeneration of time: today, conflict, famine, disease and pollution are widespread in many parts of the world; a peaceful healthy environment is rare. 2. The degeneration of beings: many people today openly follow paths that are morally wrong and indulge in gross acts of violence and sexual misconduct. 3. The degeneration of delusions: most people are motivated by delusions like greed, hatred and stupidity. 4. The degeneration of lifespan: most people have short lifespans. The causes of unnatural, untimely death are many. 5. The degeneration of views: many people come under the sway of political and religious systems where the views propagated are gross and mistaken, leading only to further suffering. Even so, these degenerate times are said to be the best for the practice of Tantra. Yet, Tantra is not meant for degenerate people.

In the Hinayana, the Buddha taught a path in which one

recognizes the five principal delusions that beset our minds—ignorance, anger, lust, pride and envy—as the chief causes of negative actions that produce suffering in this life and in future lives. Therefore, these delusions and the situations which provoke them are to be avoided under all circumstances. The path that steers clear of them is that of the Bhikshu (or Bhikshuni) where, externally, one takes on the appearance of a monk or nun, and, internally, one takes solemn vows to avoid the 'Ten Non-Virtuous Actions' that arise from these mental delusions. The 'Ten Non-Virtuous Actions' are three of the body—killing, stealing and sexual misconduct—four of speech—lying, abuse, divisive talk and idle gossip—and three of the mind—malice, covetousness and holding wrong views.

In the Mahayana, the Buddha has permitted Bodhisattvas to use the three non-virtuous actions of body and the four of speech, solely with the motive of benefiting others, such as stealing from the selfish rich to give to the needy poor, or even to kill an evil person intent on bringing harm to many others. Such actions must, however, never be motivated by the three root mental delusions—one may act with an appearance of anger but must not bear any hatred or ill-will and one must never act out of selfish reasons.

In Tantra, specially Highest Yoga Tantra, the Buddha has shown Tantric Bodhisattvas how to use the delusions rampant in this dark age as an actual path. By emanating awe inspiring lustful and wrathful forms, the Buddha has shown, through powerful symbolic means, how to use the energy of lust and anger to access subtle levels of reality which would otherwise be inaccessible to the gross level of mind.

Using the energy of lust and anger as actual paths means

that while normal human beings have many social taboos, roadblocks, one-way signs to keep anger and lust in check, a Tantric practitioner would be required to remove these checks and deliberately engage in yogas that greatly enhance the energy of lust and anger. If uncontrolled or wrongly directed, this energy could have grave consequences, both for the individual and for others. Further, if such yogic techniques are based on ego-centred, absolutist, power-hungry philosophies, not only will the individual lose hope of attaining enlightenment, but will also tighten the noose of *samsara* and deeper suffering around one's own neck. Thus, it should be clear why Tantra is a dangerous and secret path—to be taught only to mature, well-balanced individuals. Here 'maturity' specifically refers to ethical and moral maturity, and 'well balanced' means someone who has found the 'Middle Way' of behaviour, meditation and philosophy.

Moral and ethical maturity is attained when the practitioner, by following the principles of the Hinayana, engenders genuine renunciation for cyclic existence, and by practising the techniques of the Mahayana generates Bodhichitta—the altruistic aspiration to attain the enlightened state of a Buddha for the benefit of others. Renunciation is essential in order to channelize the energy of lust as a path without becoming a Hedonist, and it is necessary to have a mind filled with infinite compassion (the basis of Bodhichitta), like a mother for her only child, in order to use anger as a path without becoming a malevolent demon. Further, it is necessary to uphold the philosophical view of the 'Middle Way' which, according to the Geluk-pa, is the Prasangika Madhyamika system of Acharya Chandrakirti, disciple of Arya Nagarjuna, because that system expounds the nature of reality as it actually is.

A basic premise of Tantra is that for an ordinary (untrained) being, whenever the senses and their respective objects come into contact, the resultant sensory perception furthers the mental continuum of ignorance that grasps at reality as absolutely existent. However, for a Tantric practitioner, who has correctly understood the philosophical view of the 'Middle Way' (Madhyamika), contact between the senses and their objects ensures the continuity of the wisdom-realizing-emptiness. Then, if a sensory consciousness is blissful, it greatly enhances the wisdom-realizing-emptiness. Such a consciousness that is a union of bliss and emptiness is the principal path for actualizing the Tantric 'Ultimate Truth' of the Clear Light ground-state. But if an ignorant being, bereft of the right philosophical view, were to use the yogic bliss-enhancing techniques, it would only strengthen the continuum of ignorance, and Tantra, instead of liberating and enlightening, will accomplish the opposite. As the Tibetan Tantric adept Yeshey Gyaltsen, tutor to the Eighth Dalai Lama, says:

> It is said that the profound view of the 'middle way' is the life of both the Sutra and Tantra paths. Also, it is said that particularly with respect to Highest Secret Mantra, there is no chance of having an actual path of Mantra without this view.

Thus, it is impossible to practise Highest Yoga Tantra without having a solid foundation of renunciation, Bodhichitta and the correct view of Emptiness—the so-called 'Three Principal Aspects of the Path' put forth by Lama Tsongkhapa as a summary of the entire Sutrayana. Whereas the Buddha taught Hinayana, Mahayana and Vajrayana as separate paths in themselves, it is essential for a Tantric practitioner to integrate the practice of all three. That is why Highest Yoga Tantra is considered to be the pinnacle of Buddhist yoga and philosophy.

The rest of the chapter will focus on how to achieve renunciation, explain why Bodhichitta is the moral and ethical basis of Tantra, and define how to generate the correct view of Emptiness, in accordance with the Prasangika Madhyamika system of Acharya Chandrakirti, as the philosophical basis of Tantra.

MORAL AND ETHICAL MATURITY

The Buddhist morality is based on the acceptance and understanding of the law of karma, or cause-and-effect. According to the Buddha, this life is the effect of previous lives, and will, in turn, be the cause of future lives. Since each life in the past has been the same, a beginningless continuum of lives is implied, with no need for a 'creator' or original cause, and no place for random chance. Further, this means that the quality of life that one experiences is the direct consequence of one's past actions. Thus, the apparently 'given' constants of our lives such as our sex, appearance, intelligence, family, economic situation, nationality, environment, close relationships, friends and enemies, good and bad fortune, and the time and manner of our death, are all fixed by our actions in past lives.

An individual is thus wholly responsible for his or her condition. If this is so, it becomes imperative to know how to act so as to generate the causes of happiness and to avoid those of suffering. Realizing the need for an ethical guide, one becomes fit to take the first step on the Buddhist Tantric Path—Taking Refuge. According to the Sutra tradition, one takes Refuge in the Three Jewels—the Buddha, as the teacher; the Dharma, as the teaching; and the Sangha, or the spiritual community, as one's guide. The Buddha is a valid refuge because 'He has gone before, knows the road, and knows the goal.' As a Tantric practitioner, one, first of all, takes refuge in the Tantric guru, from whom one receives initiation and instruction, for he has attained the goal and is therefore a Buddha. His speech and actions are the authentic Dharma, and his physical presence is the valid Sangha.

It would be appropriate at the outset to lay great stress on an acceptance and, if possible, an understanding of the doctrine of karma, of past and future lives, because this is the practical basis of the entire Buddhist path in general, and of the Tantric path in particular. Without a thorough understanding of the 'mechanism' of the processes of death and rebirth, the practice of Highest Yoga Tantra is impossible. We shall discuss these processes at length in later chapters of this book, suffice it to say here that in Highest Yoga Tantra, Buddha has taught that a very subtle level of consciousness, called the 'Clear-Light Mind', and its wind-energy are the 'final basis of designation' of a person. It is the entity that is the repository of the seeds of karma; it travels from life to life, experiencing birth, ageing, death and rebirth. The entire Tantric path is basically devoted to isolating and purifying this entity of the 'Fundamental Innate Mind of Clear Light', which is bound in cyclic existence and which is liberated from such an existence.

CYCLIC EXISTENCE

In order to evoke genuine renunciation or 'the wish to be

free', it is necessary to seriously contemplate the Buddha's teaching concerning cyclic existence, technically called 'The Twelve Links of the Dependent-Arising of Cyclic Existence' (Sanskrit: *Pratitya Samutpadam Nidanam Dwadashakam*). Through contemplating these, one understands how one is bound in this cycle of suffering and how to extricate oneself from it. Just as, to understand why the sum of the squares on the two sides of a right-angled triangle equals the square on the hypotenuse, one would have to study the theorem of Pythagoras, similarly, to understand one's present existential condition, one would have to contemplate 'the twelve links', also called the 'Wheel of Existence' (Sanskrit: *Bhava Chakra*). When one's understanding of how one is bound reaches a point where the wish to be free is spontaneous, effortless, and intense, one has attained a realization of genuine renunciation.

The Bhava Chakra symbolically represents how all sentient beings, who have not practised the Dharma and liberated themselves, are bound in a cycle of existences whose very nature is suffering. The symbolism is depicted through a series of pictograms that are meant to act as a powerful mnemonic device for the serious practitioner. Such a person is advised to think about it and focus on it day and night so as never to forget its meaning. The entire ethical basis and mechanics of the Tantric path are based on an understanding of this.

THE BHAVA CHAKRA

The Bhava Chakra (Tibetan: *Srid-pe-khor-lo*) is often painted at the entrance of Tibetan Buddhist monasteries. It is also found on the walls of the Ajanta and Ellora caves, and is said to have been visualized and taught to the royal artist of king Bimbisara by the Buddha himself.

The Bhava Chakra consists of four concentric circles:

The Central Hub: The central hub consists of three components—the three main 'poisons' or natural delusions—that pollute the minds of all untrained beings and which are the prime causes of their being bound in cyclic existence: 1. Ignorance (Sanskrit: *Avidya*): Symbolically depicted by a pig, the fundamental ignorance pervades the minds of all sentient beings, from insects to Einstein, and is the root cause of cyclic existence and suffering. The Buddha has taught that just as small children are ignorant (or innocent) of adult reality, similarly, all unenlightened beings are ignorant of the true nature of reality. Specifically, this ignorance acts as an active congnitive disorder that makes us habitually misapprehend the nature of reality, just as a dreamer, overwhelmed by the dream-reality, routinely regards a dream as real and therefore experiences joy and sorrow in it. Since this ignorance is 'enemy number one' for the Tantric warrior, we shall consider it in detail in the section on 'Philosophical Maturity' (pg. 37). From ignorance arise the two other components of the central hub: 2. desire-attachment, symbolized by a rooster, and 3. anger-aversion, symbolized by a snake.

The Second and the Third Rings: Under the power of these three root-delusions, there arise '84,000 delusions', among them, malice, hatred, covetousness, dishonesty. Human beings act under their influence and thereby accumulate positive and negative karmas, as a result of which they move between high and low existences, sometimes rising to heaven

Wheel of Life
(Bhava Chakra)
Designed by Leeroy Smith

and sometimes plunging to the deepest hells. This is symbolized in the second ring which is divided into two black and white halves. The black half depicts evil persons being dragged down to the 'three lower realms', and the white half represents virtuous beings rising up to the 'three higher realms'.

These six realms of existence are then depicted in six sections of the third ring. The middle of the upper three sections depicts a scene from the Indian god Indra's 'Heaven of the Thirty-Three' (Sanskrit: *Trayatrimsa*), and represents the heavenly states of existence. These, according to Buddhist cosmology, stretch upwards from the gross sensory levels, to the subtle form-meditation levels, to the very subtle formless-meditation levels. These constitute the 'three realms' of cyclic existence called the 'Desire Realm' (Sanskrit: *Kamalok*), the 'Form Realm' (Sanskrit: *Rupalok*), and the 'Formless Realm (Sanskrit: *Arupalok*). The Buddha elaborated on these heavenly realms in order to show that the states considered to be 'Mukti' or 'Moksha' (release) from cyclic existence by the non-Buddhist systems are actually heavenly states still within cyclic existence, which eventually come to an end and the person is again reborn in lower realms. The right one of the upper three sections depicts scenes from the Asura (anti-god) realms, consisting of demonic beings, who represent the forces of darkness and are in constant conflict with the gods, who represent the forces of light. The third left section depicts the human realm.

The lower half of the third ring is divided into three sections, depicting scenes from the three 'lower realms of existence'. The section in the middle depicts scenes from the eight hot and eight cold hells that are the lowest states of existence. The right section depicts scenes from the realm of ghostly beings (Sanskrit: *Pretas*) and the left section depicts scenes from the animal realm.

These six realms constitute all possible states of existence in the universe and all beings cycle between these states, dependent on their karma, none of these states being permanent or everlasting. Thus, virtuous persons are born in heaven; virtuous beings dominated by negative emotions of jealousy are born in the anti-god (asura) realms; persons dominated by greed and attachment are born in the ghostly realms; those dominated by anger and hatred are born in hell; and those dominated by stupidity and dullness are born as animals.

The human realm is a 'middle-way' realm between the higher and lower realms. It is considered the best state of existence for practising Dharma because it is free from the constant suffering of the lower realms, and is also free of the distracting pleasures and happiness of the heavenly realms, having a bit of both. The enlightened mind appears in each of the six realms, including hell, as the 'Sage' of that realm in order to guide the beings there. Thus, it appears as Sakra among the gods, Vemachitra among the anti-gods, Sakyamuni among humans, Jwalamukhi among the Pretas (ghosts), Dhruva Simha among animals, and as Yamaraja in hell.

The Fourth Outermost Ring: This depicts in twelve pictograms the cycle of cause-and-effect that keeps beings circling in the six realms—the actual twelve links in the 'dependent origination of cyclic existence'. 1. Ignorance (Sanskrit: *Avidya*): Depicted as a blind woman about to step over an abyss, it represents a basic ignorance of the true nature of reality that keeps beings trapped in cyclic existence. Specifically, it represents ignorance in a former life which has led to the future 'projection' of this life. 2. Karma: Because of ignorance in a former life, one has committed good and evil actions that have created the karma which has resulted in this life. This is depicted by a potter working on his wheel, which keeps turning under its own momentum and forms the pot even after the impulse setting it into motion has ceased. This symbolizes how even though the person and actions of the former life have ceased, their effect 'forms' this life.

3. Consciousness (Sanskrit: *Vigyan*): When the karma-forming actions of the previous life end at death, the subtle consciousness that is the final basis of designation of a person, leaves the body and restlessly seeks the basis of another body. This is symbolized by a restless monkey. According to Highest Tantras, after leaving its former body and driven by karma, this subtle disembodied consciousness, if it is to be reborn as a human being, inevitably arrives at the place where the parents of this life are copulating. 'Riding' on the semen, it passes through the father's body into the mother's womb, where it fertilizes the ovum, and becomes the consciousness-centre of the new psychophysical complex that starts to form.

4. Name and form (Sanskrit: *Nama-rupa*): The formation of this psychophysical, or mind-body complex, that is the conventional basis of designation of a person is symbolized by two men in a boat. 5. The six sources (Sanskrit: *Shadayatana*): Once this mind-body complex becomes fully operational at birth, the six senses, i.e. the six sensory organs and their respective consciousnesses, become active as the sources of sensation. Apart from the visual,

auditory, tactile, gustatory and olfactory senses, the mind is considered the sixth sense. This is symbolized by a house with six windows. 6. Contact (Sanskrit: *Sparsh*): Once the six senses have become operational, they inevitably make contact with their respective sensory objects: eyes with visual forms, ears with sounds, nose with smells, mouth with taste, the body with tactile sensations, and the mind with feeling and thought. This is symbolized by a couple embracing. 7. Feeling (Sanskrit: *Vedana*): Once the senses come into contact with their respective objects, the mind begins discriminating between desirable, undesirable and neutral objects, depending on whether they are pleasurable, painful or neutral. This is symbolized by an arrow piercing a man's eye to emphasize the forceful and overwhelming nature of sensory reality and feeling.

8. Attachment (Sanskrit: *Trishna*): Once the mind begins discriminating among the three kinds of feelings, desire and attachment spontaneously arise for what is pleasurable. This is symbolized by a man drinking alcohol, emphasizing the addictive nature of pleasure. 9. Grasping (Sanskrit: *Upadana*): Due to the pursuit of pleasurable sensations, there is an increase in attachment to 'I' and 'mine', symbolized by a monkey grasping fruit. 10. Existence (Sanskrit: *Bhava*): Due to this grasping at this transitory mind-body and its possessions as permanent, truly existent 'I' and 'mine', one perpetuates the continuum of such an existence and 'projects' one's future life, symbolized by a pregnant woman—one's future mother. 11. Birth (Sanskrit: *Jati*): Then, at the death of this life (which is determined by actions in the past life), one's subtle consciousness again takes birth, in accordance with the causes that one has projected into the future from this life. This is depicted as a woman giving birth. 12. Ageing

and death (Sanskrit: *Jaramarana*): Then, once one is reborn in a future life, one will again inevitably undergo ageing and death, depicted as a corpse being carried to the cremation ground, and the whole cycle will be repeated again.

Thus, the first three of the twelve links have occurred in the past life, the next seven occur in this life, and the last two will occur in a future life. This means that at any given moment, one is actualizing the karmas from past lives and, simultaneously, creating new karmas, projecting a future life. Since all karmas, good and bad, are basically motivated by ignorance, one is at all times actively perpetuating the continuum of ignorance and suffering.

One should intently and seriously contemplate the meaning of this wheel. If possible, one should put up a pictorial representation of it where one can see it day and night. One should memorize the meaning and be constantly mindful of it, if necessary in solitary retreat, until its significance sinks in. Once this happens, the wish to be free of this mindless suffering is spontaneous and constant. An apt comparison would be with a sick man, who while suffering from a chronic painful ailment, discovers after a thorough medical examination that the reason for his illness is some regular component of his diet. Such a person would immediately try to remedy the defect.

Through contemplating the meaning of this wheel, one realizes that since the root cause of this continuous cycle of suffering is the fundamental ignorance that misapprehends the nature of oneself and the world, that the antidote to this ignorance is the wisdom-realizing-emptiness. And this wisdom is generated through the two-fold process of analytical reasoning and intense meditation. Then, the wish to find the exact path that leads to that wisdom is spontaneous, constant and intense. One feels the impermanence and transitoriness of life, the passing away of everything. One realizes how one's own time and energy are finite, and how sudden death can terminate this life.

Reflecting on this, one withdraws the energy and time that is invested in meaningless worldly ambitions and pleasures. Realizing how precious this time and energy are, one decides to re-invest them solely in the pursuit of the meaningful, the Dharma—in hearing it directly at the feet of gurus, in reflecting on the meaning of what has been heard and studied, and in meditating single-pointedly on the meaning understood. When this resolve reaches the point where one's interest in worldly pleasures and distractions is like the interest of a hungry lion in a bale of grass, then one has actualized a state of genuine renunciation towards cyclic existence. One enters the path of becoming a spiritual warrior, like a lotus bud about to emerge from the swamp of *samsara*. One who has actualized such a state will no longer need entertainment and titillation and will be able to live in solitude, away from time and energy-consuming relationships and tasks. As the Tibetan Tantric adept Ngulchu Thogmed Zangpo (fourteenth century A.D.) says:

> It is a practice of Bodhisattvas to remain in solitary places where (mental) obscurations gradually diminish due to the absence of harmful objects, where virtues gradually increase due to the absence of distraction, and where penetration into the meaning of Dharma arises due to clear-mindedness.

This step is crucial to ensure that one has uninterrupted time and mental energy to engage in the subtle yogas of Emptiness and Tantra which require single-minded devotion over long periods of time. It should also be clear why such a renunciation is imperative if one is to use the energy of desire and lust as an actual spiritual path. Without such renunciation, cultivating desire and lust would greatly reinforce the eighth and ninth links of the twelve links of dependent-origination (i.e. 'attachment' and 'grasping'), thereby reinforcing one's bondage to the whole cycle.

This brief analysis of the Bhava Chakra also encompasses the scope of the 'Four Noble Truths' that the Buddha has taught as the very foundation of the Buddhist spiritual path. The first and second 'Noble Truths' of True Suffering and the True Origin of Suffering are explained in detail in this wheel. Once these two are understood, the third and fourth 'Noble Truths' of the True Cessation of Suffering and the True Path that leads to that cessation is also clearly understood. For if ignorance that misapprehends the nature of reality is reversed to the wisdom that correctly understands the true nature of reality, the entire cycle of suffering, of birth-death and rebirth that arises because of that ignorance is terminated. When cyclic existence has thus been terminated, the mind of the individual abides in a continuous Samadhi (absorption) on Emptiness—the true nature of reality—and when the body of the individual disintegrates at death (determined by one's former karma), the mind continues to abide in this 'non-dual' meditative absorption and does not enter the cycle of birth-and-death. Such a state, the Nirvana, is the goal of the Hinayana.

However, this is not the aim of the Mahayana Tantric Warrior, who would, nevertheless, pay great attention to the Four Noble Truths and the Bhava Chakra because until one actualizes the Tantric 'Ultimate Truth' of the 'Clear Light' in the final Completion Stage, one is still subject to karma and to this wheel. The Tantric practitioner would conscientiously avoid the Ten Non-Virtuous Actions which are pathways to miserable lives in the three 'Lower Realms'.

This is the basis of Buddhist ethics and morality, which, in turn, is based on the dictum of 'non-harm', for the Ten Non-Virtuous Actions not only harm others but also accumulate negative karma for oneself by polluting one's mind-stream, which, from the Tantric point of view, is 'essentially pure'. The experience of suffering is like the cleansing action of the mind-stream to rid itself of pollution.

BODHICHITTA

The Mahayana Tantric guru will encourage a disciple who has attained this level of renunciation to generate the 'Mahayana Mind'—the precious Bodhichitta—that will prevent one from falling into the solitary Nirvana of a Hinayanist. The basis of this Bodhichitta is a mind filled with compassion, extending to all beings, so that one takes on the universal responsibility to deliver all sentient beings from ignorance and its resultant suffering. Thus, one enters the higher ethics of the Mahayana where, in addition to renunciation of cyclic existence and its concomitant negative principle of non-harm, one adds the positive ethics of compassionate action.

Buddha has taught that the principal enemy of the Tantric Warrior which obstructs the generation of Mahayana compassion which cherishes others more than oneself, is the deep-rooted 'self-cherishing'. This self-cherishing or ego-centrism, which holds oneself to be supreme and most important, is the product of the cognitive enemy called 'self-grasping', which clutches at the appearance of absolute existence of oneself and the objective world as true. Accustomed from past lives of ignorance, one regards phenomena to exist absolutely.

The conceptual mind which processes sensory information further grasps at this incorrect appearance of phenomena as true. This leads to the cognitive 'disorder' of dualistically apprehending the world in terms of an isolated individual versus a truly existent objective world, much as in a dream. Once this drastic, false conceptual dichotomy begins operating, the idea of 'I' and 'mine' as truly existent naturally arise and operate as ego-centred self-cherishing; the opposite of compassionate concern for others. Then, for the sake of the pleasure and well-being of this self, one engages in various negative actions such as the Ten Non-Virtues.

In order to subdue self-cherishing, Buddha has taught the techniques of 'Mind Transformation' (Tibetan: *Lo-Jong*) and to overcome self-grasping, Buddha has taught the Madhyamika philosophy. When these two—the mind-transformation techniques and the study of Madhyamika philosophy are applied simultaneously, it results in the development of the supreme and precious mind of Bodhichitta, the entrance to the Mahayana, and puts one on the path to the Complete Enlightenment of a Buddha.

🔲

SUBDUEING THE ENEMY OF SELF-CHERISHING

> '*Homage to Avolokiteshwara, who, even*
> *though he sees the lack of coming and*
> *going of all phenomena, works ceaselessly*
> *to benefit all beings.*'
>   —The Bodhisattva Thog-me Zang-po

Self-cherishing is innate to all beings and is the opposite of great compassion that cherishes others impartially. Its immediate effect on our lives is that we treasure those who are of benefit to us; we are indifferent to those who are useless to us; and hate those who are harmful to us. Thus, the entire category of 'others' gets divided into three groups—friends, neutral people and enemies. Then, in order to preserve and promote ourselves, we engage in many non-virtuous actions by hating and harming our enemies, aiding our friends and relatives, and neglecting or competing with neutral people. This attitude towards others is accepted by the worldly as 'normal' and may seem beneficial in the short-term, but in the long-term, it leads to the accumulation of negative karma that results in suffering for ourselves in future lives.

Realizing this, the Mahayana practitioner cultivates the 'Mind Transformation' techniques that originated in Tibet from the teachings of Dipankara Shri Gyan Atisha. He made these methods the core practice of the Kadampa Order, founded by his close disciple, Drom Tonpa (eleventh century). Dipankara Shri Gyan Atisha, in turn, received these teachings from Guru Dharmakirti of Suvarna-Dvipa (Sumatra) who was the lineage-holder of the teachings coming from Buddha to the Bodhisattva Maitreya (the future Buddha). In these techniques, in order to overcome self-cherishing and to nurture great impartial compassion, the practitioner cultivates a meditation that is a combination of analysis and intense visualization.

One deliberately trains one's mind to relinquish its habitual attitude of selfish concern, and to instead cultivate a sense of great indebtedness to others so that one generates the intense wish to repay the kindness of others in the best possible way by teaching them the precious Dharma that leads to omniscience and immortality. This attitude is accomplished by principally reflecting on the fact that given a beginningless and endless continuum of lives of each being, one has entered (and will enter) into every conceivable relationship with every other being. Those who are close to us today have been our bitter enemies in the past, and could become enemies again in the future. Those who are unrelated and indifferent to us, the vast majority, have been our parents and close friends in the past, even our present enemies have been and again will be our parents and friends. Reflecting on this, one initially develops a sense of equanimity and equality towards all beings. Then, by meditating on the kindness of one's parents in this life, specially on the pure selfless love of one's mother, one deliberately develops a similar sense of closeness to neutral people and enemies by imagining them as being one's mother in many past and future lives. This is cultivated in intense meditative visualization, until an actual change of heart occurs, and one can 'see' all beings as one would one's parents. Then one reflects on the suffering of these beings, of how they are all trapped in the cycle of endless birth, ageing, sickness, death, rebirth; and of how this need not be so, since there is a path to liberation and freedom.

Continuous reflection generates a strong wish to free other beings from suffering by showing them the path of release. In intense meditative sessions one visualizes taking on the suffering of other beings: this enters one's system as black smoke with each inhalation, and strikes the black knot of self-cherishing at one's heart. With each exhalation, one gives out the light of one's merit (*punya*) that relieves the suffering of all sentient beings.

In this way, one progresses from the basic Hinayana ethic of not harming others to the Mahayana ethic of an all-encompassing great compassion that wishes intensely to free all beings from suffering. As the Bodhisattva Thog-me-Zang-po says, 'Of what use is my own nirvana when all others, my own precious mothers, continue to suffer in cyclic existence?'

This Mahayana compassion progresses through three stages as delineated by Acharya Chandrakirti in his classic text *Madhyamaka-avatar* (Entry to the Middle Way). Initially, one's compassion is tainted with the fundamental ignorance that perceives oneself and others as absolutely existent entities. Acharya Chandrakirti uses the image of buckets on a wheel in a well that tumble helplessly up and down while water is being drawn up. As one's comprehension of the nature of reality deepens, one understands how we are conditioned by impermanence, transitoriness and momentariness. Chandrakirti uses the image of the reflection of the moon on rippling water to drive home the point. As one arrives at philosophical maturity through understanding the profound Madhyamika view of Emptiness, one's compassion reaches completion. Chandrakirti uses the image of the reflection of the moon on still water to explain how one's compassion for others is based on a comprehension of

Arya Nagarjuna

the true nature of reality that perceives oneself and others as lacking in absolute existence and yet appearing to exist through 'causes and conditions'.

When such an ethically mature individual resolves to attain the omniscient mind and immortal form of a Buddha, when such a resolve is cultivated through single-pointed mindfulness until it reaches a state of uncontrived spontaneity, then one has given rise to the precious mind of Bodhichitta, the gateway to the Mahayana. One then becomes a 'suitable vessel' for the 'lioness' milk' of the Tantric Dharmas.

PHILOSOPHICAL MATURITY

> *Shunyata Yasya Yujyate*
> *Tasya Sarvam Cha Yujyate*
> (For *whom Emptiness is possible,*
> *all is possible.*)
>
> —Arya Nagarjuna

In the Geluk-pa order, stress is laid on a detailed comparative study of different philosophical tenet-systems, which include both non-Buddhist and Buddhist ones. These tenet-systems are studied in a graded sequence, starting with the coarsest view and moving upward in subtlety by refuting lower systems. In this way, one is led to the 'Right View' in a stepwise manner which is considered to be extremely subtle and difficult to comprehend.

The Right View, according to the Geluk-pa order, is the philosophical concept expounded by the Buddha in the *Pragyaparamita Sutras*. Since the Buddha taught various levels of the view in different Sutras, it became necessary to single out the Buddha's actual philosophical intent. This was first accomplished by Arya Nagarjuna who established that the *Pragyaparamita Sutras* contained the subtlest explicit exposition of the view of 'self-lessness', which is the principal characteristic of Buddhist philosophy. Extracting this view from these Sutras, Nagarjuna expounded it as the basis of his Madhyamika system.

Later, while interpreting Nagarjuna's fundamental treatise, the *Mula Madhyamika Karikas*, there arose a controversy between his disciples, Bhavaviveka and Chandrakirti, whether the final view was an 'affirming negative' or a 'non-affirming negative'. In other words, since in the view of 'self-lessness', 'self' is negated, is anything positive implied by this negation or not? The answer to this question has profound implications, and Chandrakirti extensively refuted Bhavaviveka's contention that the final view was an affirming negation.

Chandrakirti established that the correct view of emptiness, according to both Buddha and Nagarjuna, is a non-affirming negation, where 'self' or 'absolute existence' is negated without residue. Acharya Chandrakirti's system came to be known as Prasangika (Consequentialist) Madhyamika because it held that no positive statement can be made about emptiness to someone who does not know it because emptiness is a non-affirming negation of 'absolute existence' with no positive implications. Acharya Chandrakirti's *Prasangika Madhyamika* was held to be supreme by all later realized Indian and Tibetan Masters and by Lama Tsongkhapa, founder of the Geluk-pa order.

All other systems which do not accord with this philosophical 'Middle Way' necessarily fall into one of the two 'extremes'—the positive extreme of Absolutism

(Sanskrit: *Atmavada, Saswatvada*) and the negative extreme of Nihilism (Sanskrit: *Uchchedavada*). The former is the implicit philosophical view held by all beings untrained in philosophy who passively accept the absolute appearance of sensory reality as being true, i.e. they accept the appearance of the world as if it existed independently of the observer, the subject. This is called 'innate ignorance', which is common to all beings, even insects and animals. When this 'given' view is taken as the foundation of complex logical systems, i.e. where logic and reasoning is used to reinforce this wrong view, it becomes 'acquired ignorance' that strengthens innate ignorance. The modern scientific materialist paradigm would fall into this category. In as much as it denies a 'Creator God', and past and future lives and karma, it would also fall into the category of moral nihilism. At a 'mind-life' conference held at His Holiness's residence in Dharamsala, where eminent Western scientists and psychologists engaged in a dialogue with His Holiness, they were perplexed by the question 'Why be good?'

Proponents of 'Creationism' who uphold that God created the world, while escaping moral nihilism (to some extent) through propounding 'divine retribution', would still fall into philosophical absolutism by asserting a truly existent world, a truly existent soul, and a truly existent God.

Higher than the materialists are the Mentalists/Idealists who assert that the Ultimate Reality is an absolutely existing mind, using terms like 'the One Mind' or 'One Without a Second' to describe this mind. They further assert that the objective world is non-existent. Although closer to the 'Middle Way', these systems nevertheless fall to both extremes. They fall to the extreme of positive Absolutism by asserting an absolutely existent Mind, and also fall to a nihilistic extreme by negating the valid existence of the objective world. They end up with a sterile monism, which is an over simplistic reduction of the objective world to the subjective, as a solution to the problem of subject-object Duality. Whereas naïve materialists try to reduce mind to matter, claiming it to be an 'epiphenomenon' of highly organized matter, the idealist systems go to the other extreme of trying to reduce the material, objective world to subjective mind.

The 'Middle Way' that avoids both these extremes does not rely on the simplistic device of reductionism, stating that subjective and objective reality validly exist as separate functional entities, and yet are the same in being mutually interdependent and, therefore, lack absolute existence. Subjective reality is called 'subjective reality' in dependence on something other than itself, i.e. 'objective reality' and vice versa. This shows that their very existence depends on something other than themselves, and therefore both subjective and objective reality are empty of absolute existence. This is their 'sameness', the 'sameness' of all phenomena, the Madhyamika resolution of Duality (and multiplicity). How the nature of subjective and objective reality, and indeed of all existents, is ontologically the 'same' is explained in the Madhyamika doctrine of the 'Two Truths'.

THE TWO TRUTHS

The profound Emptiness (Sanskrit: *Shunyata*, Tibetan: *Tong-pa-nyid*) is the philosophical and experiential core of the Buddha Dharma. It is the philosophical essence in the sense that one is first led to a comprehension of it through logical analysis involving devices like reasoning, proof and refutation. It is the experiential core because the conceptual image of Emptiness that one develops through logical analysis is the highest object to be realized in non-conceptual, direct cognition, cultivated with effort in single-pointed meditation.

In general, one becomes a Buddhist when one takes refuge from the depth of one's heart in the three Precious Jewels—the Buddha, the Dharma, and the Sangha—and one lives one's life avoiding the Ten Non-Virtues. But in order to become a Buddhist practitioner of any of the three vehicles of Hinayana, Mahayana or Vajrayana, one must become a Buddhist 'tenet-holder' (Sanskrit: *Siddhantin*). In particular, one must uphold, i.e. establish for oneself as true, the four basic axioms of Buddhism called the 'Four Seals', which determine whether a system is Buddhist or not:

1. *Dukkha* (suffering): All contaminated phenomena (i.e. the objects of consciousnesses tainted by delusions of ignorance, desire and aversion) are of the nature of suffering.
2. *Anitya* (impermanence): All compounded phenomena are impermanent, i.e. momentary (Sanskrit: *Kshanit*).
3. *Anatman* (self-less): All phenomena are self-less, i.e. empty.
4. *Nirvana*: Only the state of Nirvana, as taught by the Buddha, is the final cessation of suffering.

In accordance with the Madhyamika system of Arya Nagarjuna and Chandrakirti, which distills the essence of the *Pragyaparamita Sutras* of the Buddha, the third axiom of 'self-lessness' or Emptiness (which are synonyms) is said to be the Fundamental or Ultimate Truth (Sanskrit: *Paramartha Satya*). Whereas the other three axioms apply only to limited classes of phenomena at certain times, the third axiom applies to all phenomena at all times, i.e., all existent phenomena of the past, present and future are empty or self-less. Further, this Emptiness is called the Ultimate Truth not because it ultimately or absolutely exists (which it does not), but because it is the ultimate or highest object of knowledge, since realization of it is the cause of the attainment of the highest state of existence i.e. Nirvana and Buddhahood.

This Emptiness is also called 'Fundamental Truth' because it is the final actual mode of existence of all phenomena. In relation to this Emptiness, all other phenomena which are the bases of the quality of Emptiness, are called 'Conventional Truths' (Sanskrit: *Samvriti-Satya*). Thus, all existent beings or things such as persons, houses, mountains, planets, space, molecules, thoughts, ideas and expressions are Conventional Truths, or provisional truths, and their actual mode of existence, their Emptiness, is the Ultimate or Fundamental Truth.

Each and every knowable phenomenon has this dual nature—its conventional nature which consists of its attributes such as colour, shape, mass by which it is known, and its ultimate nature, which is Emptiness. Whereas manifest phenomena, i.e. Conventional Truths, can be directly cognized by the sensory consciousnesses and minds of ordinary beings, their Emptiness or ultimate nature is a 'hidden', 'subtle' object. The existence of this Emptiness can only be inferred indirectly, and can only be cognized by a special subtle, single-pointed meditative consciousness developed by yogis in meditative equipoise (Sanskrit: *Samadhi, Samahit*).

So what is this Emptiness, this Ultimate Truth, which is the most fundamental fact about all phenomena? And why is its knowledge so crucial?

In the *Pragyaparamita Sutras* of the Mahayana canon, the Buddha has taught that all phenomena, both animate and inanimate, are empty of or lack a certain specific quality which, nevertheless, appears to the minds and senses of all untrained beings. He called this quality 'self' (Sanskrit: *Atma*) and stated that all phenomena are self-less and therefore empty. The Buddha used examples like mirages, illusions, dreams and hallucinations to illustrate what he meant by the term 'self-less', in that these phenomena appear to possess a reality which they lack. He then used extensive reasoning to establish that even though phenomena appeared to possess a 'self', in actual terms they lacked such a self. This 'self' is called the 'object of negation', and the whole view of Emptiness depends on understanding exactly and precisely what this object of negation is. As Aryadeva, a close disciple of Arya Nagarjuna, says 'Without understanding the object to be negated, it is impossible to understand its absence.'

According to the Prasangika Madhyamika system of Acharya Chandrakirti, which is considered to be supreme by the Geluk-pa school of Tibetan Buddhism, this 'self' or object of negation means 'absolute existence', 'true existence', 'independent existence', 'existence independent of thought and conceptual designation', 'self-defining existence' and 'existence independent of the observer'. This object of negation is not a philosophical fabrication but the 'normal' way in which all of us perceive the world.

To us, everything appears to exist absolutely, as if completely independent of our perception and thought processes. Because everything appears to have this absolutely real existence, we experience feelings like desire, aversion, fear or anger towards these phenomena, just as a man experiences fear on mistaking a rope for a snake in the dark. Because of these feelings, we act in the world and accumulate karmas that result in future lives and, in this way, we are caught in the cycle of *samsara*. Out of habit, not only do phenomena appear to our senses to be truly existent, but we also actively grasp at this appearance of absolute existence as true. This is what the Buddha calls 'self-grasping'—the greatest enemy and mother of 'self-cherishing'[1]—the root of our suffering.

Like children in an amusement park, we are enthralled by the appearance of the sensory world. Since it appears to truly exist, we passively accept this false appearance as a 'given'. And then in a deeply ingrained, instinctive response, we crave pleasure and shun pain. Seeking pleasure, we are unable to always get what we want, and even if we get it, we are surprised when it trickles out of our fingers like water. Wanting to avoid pain and unpleasant circumstances, we are unable to do so, and thus we suffer, trying to grasp at the ungraspable, ephemeral and empty world. To us, the world seems to be the opposite of what it actually is—it appears to absolutely exist whereas it actually lacks, is empty of, this absolute existence. Not realizing this profound emptiness, we are forced to cocoon ourselves in an over-concretized selfhood, and then its finite 'me' versus the infinite world. That suffering will ensue is inevitable.

Therefore, realization of this profound Emptiness is crucial and indeed is the sole pathway to liberation. As Sutra says, 'Through no other means does one come to peace.'

REALIZING EMPTINESS

In understanding and realizing the profound Emptiness, the trainee progresses through seven steps:

1. Wrong view
2. Doubt tending to the wrong view
3. Two-pointedness
4. Doubt tending to the right view
5. Correct assumption
6. Inferential cognition
7. Direct cognition.

The process can analogically be explained thus: imagine you have an old trusted friend who pervades every aspect of your life. You have implicit faith in him/her and are ready to trust your very life and property to such a friend. Then imagine if a well-wisher one day warns you, telling you that you are being deceived and that your 'friend' is planning to harm you greatly. At first, you react with disbelief, but since the seeds of doubt have been sown, you perhaps look for proof. Then if your well-wisher were to show you incontrovertible proof of your 'friend's' duplicity, you may reach an 'inferential cognition' of your friend's real nature even though, externally, things remain the same. Then imagine, if after laying a careful trap, you were to catch your friend red-handed in trying to harm you; that would be like 'direct cognition'.

Initially, one has no understanding, and one begins with the view that we and our world truly, absolutely exist, an impression which one shares with all sentient beings untrained in the right view. Then through contact with teachings on Emptiness, one, for the first time, begins to doubt the 'givenness' of the world, but since one's understanding of the 'object of negation' is poor and one's attention span is limited, one mostly reverts to one's habitual way of viewing the world as absolutely real. However, it is said that once the process of comprehension begins, it has a snowballing effect and as Aryadeva says, 'It tears *samsara* to shreds.' As one's attention span stabilizes, the 'object of negation' becomes increasingly clear, and through the intense application of the 'Five Great Logical Devices' of the Madhyamikas[2], one realizes its impossibility, its utter negation and absence.

The trainee usually begins with an obvious, tangible object like a car (in the ancient texts, a chariot). One analyses whether the car, which seems to have an 'objective' existence as if it existed right there as the possessor of its parts, completely independent of the observer's thought processes, really exists the way it appears. If such a car existed, it would have to exist as being one with or other than its parts, there being no third possibility. It cannot be found as being one with its parts, because the parts are plural whereas the car is singular, and singularity and plurality are mutually exclusive. It cannot be found as being other than the parts, because a car without parts is impossible. It is also not the collection of the parts because there is no such 'thing' as a collection.

The question would again arise whether the 'collection', which is singular (as in 'a collection'), is one with or other than the car's parts. Similarly, none of the parts (which are composite objects), right down to the smallest bolt, can be found under analysis as being either one with or other than its parts. Under such an analysis, nothing can be found— persons, bodies, brains, neurons, theories, paradigms,

Buddhas, Dharma, paths, results, universes, beings, space or time. Does this mean that phenomena are non-existent?

All beings other than Prasangika Madhyamikas are unable to distinguish between 'absolute existence' and 'mere existence'. Therefore, when the Buddha says that phenomena do not absolutely exist, non-Madhyamikas think he means that phenomena do not exist at all. Then, to save beings from nihilism, when the Buddha says that phenomena do validly exist as functioning things, the non-Madhyamikas think he means that phenomena exist as we perceive them i.e. absolutely. These are the 'Two Extremes'—the positive philosophical extreme of Absolutism which confuses functional existence to mean absolute existence, and the negative philosophical extreme of Nihilism that confuses the negation of absolute existence with total non-existence. The Middle Way (Madhyamika) is that philosophical position which utterly refutes both these extremes.

So, if a truly existent car cannot be found under analysis, how does a car exist? In order to answer this question, one must rely on the 'King of Reasonings'—'Dependent-existence' (Sanskrit: *Pratityasamutpada*) which states, 'Phenomena are empty of absolute existence because they exist dependently.' The first part of this statement (phenomena are empty of absolute existence) refutes the positive extreme and the second part (because they exist dependently) refutes the negative extreme. Also, the first part refutes the negative extreme because only 'absolute existence' is negated, not existence in general. The second part also refutes the positive extreme because phenomena are stated to be dependent-existents which is the opposite of absolute, independent existence.

Phenomena are said to be dependent-existents because

first, they exist in dependence on phenomena other than themselves, for example, a car (or any other phenomena) exists in dependence on its parts (all of which are 'non-cars'). Secondly, a phenomenon exists in dependence on its 'basis of designation' (the 'whole' that appears to the mind). Thirdly, it exists in dependence on the designation (car), and fourthly, and most important, it exists in dependence on the designating consciousness which is familiar with the convention of a 'car'. Only when all these factors come together can a car or any phenomenon be said to be existent, for in the absence of even one of them, it would be impossible to establish the existence of anything.

The crucial point is that all phenomena finally owe their existence to the consciousness of the perceiver. If one were to search for any phenomenon as existing independently of the observer's thought processes, which is the way that phenomena appear to exist, one would be unable to find it. This unfindability is the Emptiness of all phenomena. It does not mean the non-existence of phenomena, but the existence of all phenomena in dependence on thought (learned conventions). Not understanding this crucial and subtle point, the non-Buddhist Indian philosopher, Adi Shankaracharya (eighth century A.D.), dismissed Nagarjuna as a complete nihilist and therefore unworthy of refutation. I suspect that he did this because he realized that Nagarjuna is irrefutable. As Nagarjuna himself says (paraphrased)—

If I had a thesis asserting true existence
I would be subject to refutation,
Because I alone have no thesis asserting true existence
I alone am irrefutable.

After becoming familiar with the mode of analysis and its implications, using a solid tangible object like a car, the yogi then turns one's attention to oneself. In intense, single-pointed analytical meditation, one mentally recalls the object of negation with respect to oneself. One clearly sees how 'I' appears to be absolutely existent, as if I am a findable, pointable entity, definitely existing right here (somewhere in the centre of the chest, or if you are a brain-is-me proponent, then somewhere behind your eyes).

In order to make the object of negation clearer, the yogi recalls a shameful or embarrassing incident, or when one was wrongly accused or treated badly, and one watches the strong sense of the 'I' that arises. Is this tangible, palpable 'me' the body or some organ or physical system? One then examines to see if either the body or any of its organs can be found under analysis so that it could be 'me'. The yogi searches intensely, 'from the top of one's head to the soles of one's feet', to see if any entity can withstand analysis and be 'found' as being this apparently truly existent 'me'. The yogi will discover (perhaps with a shock) that neither the body as a whole, nor any of its individual parts, or physical systems down to the last strand of DNA, can be found as truly existing 'findable' entities, independent of the observer.

So, if I am not the tangible physical body, I must be the intangible mind that seems to inhabit this body. One then analyses to see if any of the 'four aggregates of mind' taught by the Buddha as being the 'components' of the mind can be found under analysis. One analyses whether feelings, ideas, conditioning or consciousness can be found under examination. For the lay meditator, this is a moment of shock and fear, as if one has been robbed. One fails to find a locus of the self ('I') in the only two places where it could be found—body and mind. Further, since body and mind cannot be found individually, there is no possibility of finding a truly existent 'collection of body and mind' to identify with. It is as if one has been thrown into bottomless space.

For the Prasangikas, this unfindability of the self does not mean that 'I' am non-existent. That is the nihilistic extreme. This unfindability only means that an absolutely existent 'I', as conceived by the mind to be the possessor of mind and body, is non-existent. Such an absolutely existent 'I' is negated without residue. However, the mere concept 'I', based on the appearance of a valid basis of designation of mind and body, is not thereby negated.

The yogi does not fall to an extreme of Nihilism because, mindful of the Buddha's core 'slogan' of 'dependent existence' (*Pratityasamutpada*), the yogi realizes that emptiness means dependent existence. In other words, 'I' exist in dependence on 'my' components—mind and body— and the thought that thinks 'I' when the mind-body complex appears as a 'whole', that is as the basis of designation of 'me'. Further, the mind and body are also dependent existents that are mere conceptual labels given by a designating consciousness. In this way, the yogi, through understanding the emptiness of one thing, is able to understand the universal emptiness of all things.

The yogi understands that even though phenomena continue to appear as if they existed absolutely, concretely, independent of the perceiver's consciousness, this appearance is an exaggeration, superimposed by the ignorant mind onto phenomena. It is not a trait inherent in phenomena themselves, much as the reality and concreteness of dream-phenomena are an exaggeration superimposed by the ignorant mind of the dreamer, and not a characteristic of the dream-phenomena themselves.

In this way, the yogi subjects all classes of phenomena to analysis. Over a long period of familiarizing one's mind with the vast implications of this analysis, one progresses through seven steps to cognizing Emptiness. When one arrives at a correct understanding of the 'object of negation' (absolute existence), and through analysis realizes its complete absence in all phenomena even though it appears to the mind, then one has begun to arrive at a correct, logically derived assumption about the nature of reality.

When the yogi can clearly understand that the unfindability of phenomena does not negate their valid functional existence, like dream objects, one arrives at the sixth step of 'inferential cognition'. At that time, the yogi's mind is able to conceive an internal mental image of the emptiness of all phenomena, even though they continue to appear as truly existent as always. This clear internal mental image of emptiness then becomes the focus of intense meditative stabilization (Sanskrit: *Shamatha*), combined with analytical meditation, where the analysis reinforces the focus and vice versa in a technique called 'Vippassana'. This is where the Tantric path separates from that of the Sutras. Although the image of Emptiness arrived at through logical analysis remains the object of meditative focus, the meditative techniques of Tantra differ vastly in their scope from those taught by the Buddha in the non-Tantric vehicle of the Sutras.

The gap between the sixth step of inferential cognition, and the seventh step of direct cognition of emptiness, is a vast one. It can only be bridged by intensive Vippassana meditation. The reason for this is that inferential cognition of Emptiness is dualistic where the sense of a meditator and an object meditated upon remain. Having understood how the world and the self (I) appear to be absolutely existent to the senses and the mind, one concludes, on the basis of reasoning, that this appearance of absolute existence is mistaken, is impossible, like mistaking dream objects for real when one is overwhelmed by the dream-reality.

Thus, although the world and the self ('I'), out of a deeply ingrained habit, continue to appear as absolutely existing, one realizes how this appearance is deceptive. Technically, one would then have negated, without remainder, the object of negation i.e. absolute existence. The world will continue to appear as it always did, but in one's mind one would have generated a correct image of how the world actually is—an image of an empty but functional world. This image of emptiness is the object of meditation.

If one is a Hinayanist by motivation, i.e. if one seeks an immediate cessation of suffering in a personal Nirvana, one would mentally focus on this image of the emptiness of oneself in intense Vippassana meditation. This is described as a union of single-pointedness and analytical scrutiny— until the dualistic conceptual image of emptiness disappears, and one attains a direct, non-dual cognition of the emptiness of all phenomena. This is the state where the mind of the meditator and the Ultimate Truth of Emptiness are merged like space in a glass mixing with the space outside when the glass is broken. At that time, one would become an Arya (noble being) and surpass all beings in cyclic existence, even gods like Brahma.

After repeated meditation, one would attain a direct cognition of Emptiness—described as space-like, akin to the to the clear colourless autumn sky just before the sun rises. Then, when the body of the meditator, which is the effect of past ignorant karma, dies according to its karmically determined end, the meditator (Arhat) remains in this timeless space-like cognition of Emptiness indefinitely—the state of Nirvana—the cessation of sorrow and rebirth.

A Mahayanist does not aspire to a personal Nirvana because one is then of no use to others. Motivated by great compassion, ready to work ceaselessly to deliver all beings from cyclic existence, the Mahayanist realizes that the doctrine of the Two Truths teaches that the two truths—Emptiness, the Ultimate Truth, and all other phenomena, the Conventional Truths—are actually one entity but appear as different to a dualistic mind.

Ordinary people are aware of only Conventional Truths, but do not cognize Ultimate Truth. Hence, they fall into the extreme of *samsara*. Hinayana Arhats, on the other hand, perceive only Ultimate Truth and not conventional phenomena and thereby fall into the extreme of personal Nirvana. However, since Ultimate and Conventional Truths are actually one entity, like two sides of a coin, it is possible to cognize them simultaneously, in one moment of consciousness. Such a cognition would necessarily be omniscient, i.e. to such a consciousness, the emptiness of all phenomena and all phenomena themselves would appear simultaneously. The attainment of this omniscient consciousness, which is a 'union of the Two Truths', is the final aim of the Buddha-Dharma; it is what is called the state of Complete Enlightenment (Sanskrit: *Samma-Sambodhi*).

In the Mahayana Sutras, a gradual path spanning 'Three Countless Aeons of Time' is taught in order to attain the omniscient state of Complete Enlightenment. During this period, the Bodhisattva practitioner accumulates not just the wisdom of Emptiness but also vast 'collections' of merit (Punya) in order to surmount the 'obstruction to omniscience' (Sanskrit: *Gye avarana*) which prevents the mind from perceiving all phenomena simultaneously. This vast 'collection' of 'Punya' and 'Pragya' (the transcendent wisdom of Emptiness) is accomplished through the practice of the 'Six Perfections' (Sanskrit: *Paramitas*) of generosity, patience, ethics, enthusiastic perseverance, meditation and wisdom.

The Bodhisattva practitioner cultivates single-pointed cognition of Emptiness in formal meditation sessions. In the post-meditation period, one works for the benefit of others by practising generosity and patience, constantly mindful that the 'three spheres' of subject, object, and action are all empty of true existence. In this way, one gradually ascends the Ten Bodhisattva levels (Sanskrit: *Bhumis*), over a vast continuum of lives, until eventually one arrives at the tenth Bhumi. But in order to attain the omniscience of Complete Enlightenment, it would still be necessary to enter the Path of Highest Yoga Tantra.

It is not possible to attain Complete Enlightenment without practising Highest Yoga Tantra. This is because, at present, our mind and body are gross which is the effect of past ignorant karma. A gross mind like ours is necessarily dualistic, therefore it is impossible for it to attain all-pervasive omniscience. The omniscient mind can be attained by generating a very subtle level of mind, called 'The Fundamental Innate Mind of Clear Light'. This can be achieved through techniques taught in Highest Yoga Tantra. These methods are not taught in the non-Tantric vehicle of the Sutras which can only lead one up to the tenth Bodhisattva Bhumi. However, it is not necessary to ascend to the tenth Bhumi before entering the practice of Tantra. One can enter the Tantric vehicle anytime after one has attained an inferential cognition of Emptiness, provided one has sufficient experience of the other two prerequisites of renunciation and Bodhichitta.

In the advanced meditative methods of Tantra, called the techniques of 'overwhelming means', the grosser levels of mind, which are conceptual and dualistic, are forcefully stopped. The very subtle levels of mind can then become manifest, just as a total solar eclipse stops the sun's light so that the subtle light of the stars can become manifest during the day. These techniques imitate the internal process that occurs naturally at death so that the meditator experiences the death-state while still alive. These yogas can only be practised by someone who has a firm and stable personality attained through the deliberate cultivation of ethical and philosophical maturity. As His Holiness the Dalai Lama often says, if one practises the vehicle of the Sutras without Tantra, there is no harm, one can only benefit, but if one practises the path of Tantra without the firm foundation of Sutra, there is only harm, no benefit.

Note: Although the above discussion about the profound Emptiness is sufficient as a starter, the serious seeker is advised to search for a more detailed, definitive, incontrovertible understanding, based on a detailed study of authentic texts by Indian and Tibetan Masters, and to seek out commentaries on these texts by living masters and lineage-holders. One should not begin meditating on Emptiness until one has presented one's understanding of it to a Master and had it confirmed as correct. Otherwise, one may be meditating on something other than the actual Emptiness, with grave consequences for oneself. It may lead to rebirth as a dim-witted human being or as an animal.

▣

3. Tantric World View

'. . . The goal of expressions is beyond expression
The goal of ideas is non-conceptuality
The goal of consciousness is perfect and
*   complete cognition*
And the goal of this apparition of reality
*   is reality itself.'*
—H.H. Dudjom Rimpoche

THE TANTRIC WORLD view, as presented in the highest Tantras, is final—the summation of the Buddha's teachings. According to the Tibetan traditions, the Tantras are directly revealed by the omniscient mind itself, using powerful symbolic imagery and coded expressions. These have many levels of meaning, and deal with the very subtle class of phenomenon that are beyond our sensory experience, beyond all thought and expressions, and beyond the ken of dualistic gross minds.

The gurus do not teach the Tantras to those who merely have an academic interest in them, but only instruct those yogis and yoginis who are firm in their intent to follow the path. Logical devices such as proof and refutation are dispensed with (although they are used in determining the meaning of the texts), and a vision of reality is presented from the point of view of the resultant state. Paths that are in accordance with that state are then taught to the practitioner for personal experience and not for mere intellectual speculation.

Thus, the entities spoken of in Tantra, such as deities, drops, channels, mandalas and chakras, are not objects whose existence can be established by logical analysis or by modern, scientific devices, which merely deal with the gross material class of phenomenon. The existence of these entities can only be established by direct personal experience, cultivated in intense meditative states that generate subtle levels of consciousness, which have the capacity to directly comprehend these objects. In any case, as His Holiness says, it does not matter whether these entities exist or not, as long as meditating on them produces the required effect.

THE DOCTRINE OF THE THREE BODIES (TRIKAYA)

In Tantra, the true nature of reality is spoken of as being primordially and completely pure, a spontaneously present mandala (system) of Enlightened awareness, which is imaginary in that it does not truly exist and is like a dream. Perfectly present down to the minutest detail, it is free of even the slightest taint. Beyond time, thought and symbolism, completely insubstantial and free of truly existent materiality, the true nature of reality is beyond all dualistic categories of subject or object, good or evil and beautiful or ugly. This sphere of perfect cognition is exclusively the domain of enlightened Buddhas, and its nature is described as being that of 'uncontaminated Great Bliss'.

Simultaneously existing at three levels, like the three

levels of the great ocean (surface, middle, and the deep), the three levels of this spontaneously present mandala are the formless Dharmakaya or 'Body of Phenomena' which is the omniscient awareness that perceives all pure and impure phenomena of *samsara* and Nirvana as being of 'one taste' (same ontological status). This greatly blissful, non-dual awareness appears in a perfect empty form which is called the Sambhogakaya or 'Body of Perfect Rapture' and is described as the 'Sambhogakaya mandala' of the Five Tathagatas and their five consorts and retinues.[1]

This fundamental mandala further appears as the countless mandalas of the various levels of Tantra in order to instruct appropriate disciples such as eighth ground Bodhisattvas and above, gods such as Rudra and Bhairava, and Tantric yogis and yoginis. Then, in all the six realms of cyclic existence, including countless worlds like ours which are called the 'field of activity' (Sanskrit: *Nirmana*) of the third level of this mandala, it appears in the form of the Buddhas and gurus of flesh and blood called the Nirmanakaya or 'Body of Development'. They guide beings in their karmic activity so that they too can become enlightened by directly perceiving this fundamentally pure expanse of reality.

These illusory imaginary beings (us), who constitute the 'field of activity' of the Nirmanakayas of all the Buddhas, have imaginary minds contaminated by imaginary ignorance and delusions. Their individual consciousnesses span every infinite possibility of dualistic awareness, from High Gods like Brahma, to gods of the Desire Realm like Rudra and Indra, to demons, humans, animals, ghosts and beings from hell. These imaginary beings regard this imaginary mandala as a truly existent world in conformity with the conventions of their own realms, and within that, in accordance with their own individual karma. Trying to grasp this illusory appearance as real, they circle in an ostensible cycle of suffering.

The Buddhas, out of great compassion, manifest as the very 'stuff' of the imaginary universe—space, time, matter, energy and consciousness—and allow for the infinite combinations and recombinations of these elements as infinite worlds. The particular features of each age in the world are determined by the collective karma of sentient-beings in a previous world-age, and the enlightened activity of the Nirmanakayas of Buddhas, who appear effortlessly to guide them in accordance with their karma. Thus, reality as we experience it, is, in a sense, the interface between the enlightened activity of Buddhas and the ignorant collective karma of sentient beings.

BUDDHA NATURE IN TANTRA

This tri-fold mandala of the Three Bodies (Sanskrit: *Trikaya*)—the Dharmakaya, the Sambhogakaya, and the Nirmanakaya[2]—is experienced by humans as the three states of deep sleep, dreaming and waking in the daily cycle of their lives. It is also experienced as the three states of death, intermediate state between death and rebirth, and rebirth in the long-term cycle of their lives. Deep sleep and death (and the fourth occasion of sexual orgasm) correspond to the Dharmakaya; dreaming and the intermediate state are similar to the Sambhogakaya; and waking and rebirth correspond to the Nirmanakaya. As long as we remain ignorant sentient beings without control, these three bodies will continue to manifest in this manner. However, these three states of waking, dreaming and deep sleep, which are within our immediate daily experience and are actually the presence of the Three Bodies in us, are sought to be transformed in Tantra. The means to do this is the Tantric Path, and the results of the transformation are the Three Bodies of a fully enlightened Buddha.

Through gaining complete control over the three states of waking, dreaming and deep sleep, the yogi attains total control of the three deeper states of death, intermediate state and rebirth by transforming them into the Trikaya. Thereby, one becomes complete master of one's own destiny, with the freedom to live or die as and when one wishes, in whatever form or forms one desires. Also, in accordance with the wishes of sentient beings, one attains the ability to benefit and guide them over the continuum of their lives. The natural presence of these threefold contaminated states in our lives is one aspect of our 'Buddha Nature' (Sanskrit: *Sugata garbha, Tathagata garbha*) because these states are the potential basis for our transformation into Buddhas.

The actual Buddha Nature, according to Tantra, is the presence within each individual of the 'Fundamental Innate Mind of Clear Light', and its associated 'wind' or energy. The two are the subtlest basis of designation of a person and are the actual 'substances' that become the Dharmakaya and Rupakaya, respectively, of the resultant state. The grosser levels of mind and their associated energies originate temporarily from the subtle mind-energy and are absorbed back into it. This absorption occurs reversibly during the waking-dreaming-deep sleep cycle and occurs irreversibly during the death-intermediate state-rebirth cycle.

Thus, whereas the grosser levels of mind-energy arise and cease in a cyclic manner, the Fundamental Innate Mind of Clear Light and its energy-wind abide continuously throughout one's life. They continue from life to life, as the final basis of designation of a person. Further, since all phenomena exist merely through designation by thought (i.e. they are empty of true existence), and thought is a characteristic of grosser, dualistic minds which arise temporarily from this Fundamental Innate Mind of Clear Light, the latter is said to be the originator of all phenomena, including oneself and one's world. It can do this because it too is by nature empty and, therefore, has the freedom of the expanse of emptiness. It is like the root of certain plants which remains alive throughout all seasons. Year after year, it produces sprouts in spring which grow, flower, seed and die while the root remains constant underground.

Similarly, the Fundamental Innate Mind of Clear Light abides continuously as the final basis of designation of each and every being, whether good or evil. This, our deepest common nature, is our Buddha Nature. In the highest Tantric texts, it is spoken of as being present as a tiny seed-like 'drop' in a vacuole at the centre of the 'heart-chakra'. This all-pervasive drop of light is our Buddha Nature because if left untended and unrecognized, it produces, life after life, the poison plant of the mandala of ignorance and suffering. If recognized and carefully tended through intense Tantric meditation, it eventually produces the vast Bodhi tree of the mandala of the Trikaya of a Completely Enlightened Buddha. Its root is the Dharmakaya, the stem is the Sambhogakaya, and its myriad leaves are the Nirmanakaya which arise continuously to benefit and guide sentient-beings. Recognizing the presence of this drop of Clear Light in every being can also be a powerful method of generating the all-encompassing mind of Great Compassion— Bodhichitta.

The nature and qualities of this Fundamental Innate Mind of Clear Light is one of the principal subjects of the highest class of Tantras. This mind, when sealed with the Cognition of Emptiness and Great Bliss, is referred to as the 'Ultimate Truth' since it is the basis of all phenomena and of the Fundamental Mandala of the Rupakaya. The Rupakaya itself, which arises from the very subtle wind-energy of the Clear-Light Mind, is the other principal subject-matter of the Highest Tantras, and is referred to as the 'Conventional Truth'. As mentioned earlier, Tantras which principally emphasize the techniques for generating the 'Ultimate Truth' of the Clear Light are called Mother Tantras, and those that stress the methods for generating the Rupakaya are called the Father Tantras. The goal of both categories of Tantras is to lead the practitioner to attain the state of 'union' (Sanskrit: *Yuganaddha*) of those Two Truths—the Dharmakaya and the Rupakaya.

THE SUBTLE TANTRIC PSYCHO-PHYSIOLOGY OF BIRTH AND DEATH—THE CHANNELS, DROPS AND WINDS

According to the Highest Tantras, each person's body has a system of 72,000 channels which form the underlying subtle energy-body of each individual. Through these channels course the wind-energies, which are the mounts of the gross sensory conceptual minds. These channels converge on (or radiate out of) a central channel system that lies parallel to and in front of the spinal chord. This extends from the centre of the forehead, curves up parallel to the dome of the skull, and runs straight down to the sexual region. The blue-coloured central channel is the axis of the whole energy system. Called the channel of non-duality, it is also referred to as Avadhuti (the one that 'shakes off' duality), and Rahu (the mythical demon that periodically swallows the sun and moon, causing eclipses).

To the right and left of the central channel run two side-channels, called the left channel and the right channel, or Lalana the sun, and Rasana the moon, respectively. These are called the channels of duality with the right, red female channel being the channel of the subject, and the left, white male channel being the channel of objective reality. When the wind-energies, bearing consciousness, course through these two channels as in waking, then, because of the movement of the winds, there appears the separation between the subject and the objective world that is called Duality. These two side-channels move parallel to the central channel and coil around it in knots at several points, causing the central channel to constrict and radiate outwards in wheels (chakras) that radiate out like spokes of an umbrella.

The four principal chakras are located in the centre of the cranium behind the eyes, in the centre of the throat, in the centre of the chest, and just behind the navel. The three secondary chakras are located at the forehead, at the base of the spine, and the tip of the sexual organ. These chakras then radiate outwards, dividing and subdividing into the 72,000 channels that pervade the body.

Through these chakras and channels course the five principal and five secondary wind-mind pairs which are responsible for cognizing specific aspects of subjective and objective reality. The five principal winds are responsible for the five vital functions of breathing, digestion, movement, speech, and the voiding of waste, menstruation and ejaculation. These winds are also responsible for the cognition of the five elements of earth (solidity), water (liquidity), fire (heat and energy), wind (motion) and space in one's internal body and external world. In other words, we experience these elemental components of the physical world because of the functioning of these wind-minds.

The five secondary winds are responsible for the cognitive function of the five physical senses. In this way, when we are alive and awake, all these energies are coursing outwards from the chakras and the two side channels, causing the dualistic appearance of a karmically determined subjective and objective world.

The movement of these winds is also responsible for the movement of the two kinds of drops (Sanskrit: *Bindu*, Tibetan: *Thigle*)—the 'red drops' which derive from the original ovum from one's mother, and the 'white drops' which come from the original sperm of one's father. The white drop from one's father has its principal seat in the head-chakra. It is responsible for the waking state and for the 'melting bliss' of sexual arousal, and forms the male 'pole' of one's body. The principal seat of the red drop from one's mother is at the navel-chakra, which is the female 'pole' of the body, and which functions to produce the warmth of the body, the heat of sexual arousal and orgasm, and the digestion of food. Also located at the throat-chakra, the red drop is responsible for the dream state.

Equal portions of the red and white drops from one's parents are located at the heart-chakra, where they form an 'amulet' containing the indestructible, Fundamental Innate Mind of Clear Light and its very subtle wind-energy, that have come from previous lives. This very subtle Clear Light wind-mind couple located in the heart-chakra is the basis of this life, of consciousness, of the objects of consciousness, and of the state of deep sleep. All the principal and secondary wind-mind couples arise from it and absorb back into it reversibly in the waking-dreaming-deep-sleep cycle and irreversibly at death.

The movement of the secondary and subsidiary winds in the many channels is also responsible for the movement of fluids of the body such as blood, semen, urine and menstrual flow. Control over the movement of these wind-mind couples, drops, and their associated functions is one of the principal purposes of the Completion Stage of Highest Yoga Tantra. Although men and women differ functionally in their physical bodies, their subtle body of channels, drops and winds is identical. Therefore, both sexes are equally capable of traversing the Tantric Path to Complete Enlightenment.

DEATH

Within the context of this subtle system of channels, drops and winds, the Highest Tantras describe the death process in detail, both its objective and subjective aspects. They show how the continuum of consciousness of the Clear-Light Mind and its wind-energy are uninterrupted throughout the process of death, intermediate state and rebirth. These detailed descriptions, when authenticated through even partial experience in meditation, are the most compelling reasons which establish the continuum of past and future lives, of karma and rebirth.

According to the Tantras, when a human being dies a normal death (i.e. not a sudden or accidental one), then the karmic energy that has propelled his life runs out and the energy-winds coursing through the various channels begin imploding inwards, absorbing back into their original source—the Fundamental Innate Clear-Light Mind and its energy-wind.

A serial collapse of the consciousnesses associated with these winds occurs as the gross wind-minds subside into the subtle, and then the subtle into the very subtle. In other words, the basis of designation of a person begins to shift irreversibly from the gross physical body and mind to the subtle energy-body and mind, and eventually to the very subtle Clear-Light mind-energy. The untrained person does not realize what is happening, and as the senses and mind cease and become more subtle, one feels as if one is being annihilated into nothingness. As a result, one desperately grasps at a tangible reality and then, in accordance with one's karma, one rebounds back into *samsara*.

In death, first the earth-wind which supports consciousness of solidity absorbs and ceases. Externally, one feels one's body becoming inert and heavy, and internally, one sees a vision of a shimmering mirage. Next the water-wind absorbs and ceases, heart and blood flow stop, and the liquids in one's body begin drying up. A deafening silence arises as one can no longer hear even the constant hum hummm sound in one's ears. Internally, one sees a vision like space filled with dense swirling smoke. Following this, the fire-wind absorbs and ceases and one's body becomes cold and clammy, digestion stops, one can no longer smell, and one cannot remember names of friends and close relatives. Internally, a vision of swirling light-drops which look like fireflies arises. Then the air-wind absorbs and ceases, one stops breathing with a last exhalation, one can no longer experience taste or remember one's work, name and purpose. Internally, one sees a vision like a flickering candle flame about to go out. The gross sensory mind and its world cease and gross conceptuality comes to a halt as the gut-level instinctive conceptual patterns (called the

'Eighty Indicative Conceptions'), which consist of both virtuous and non-virtuous minds, slowly cease.

What is the last conceptual thought in the mind is important as this has a bearing on one's future life. The last conceptual thought of a virtuous person, trained in Dharma, could be one of compassion or emptiness or devotion to one's guru or the Three Precious Jewels, whereas an untrained person's last thought could well be of fear, hatred, dishonesty or other negative minds to which one is well accustomed. This determines the first conceptual mind to arise in the reverse order as one rises from the profound swoon of death, and this would be a factor in deciding one's future rebirth.

As the last conceptual mind ceases, with the winds having by now withdrawn from the extremities of the body towards the heart-chakra, and as these winds withdraw into the central channel, the two main side channels become deflated and the chakra-knots begin to unravel. The first chakra to unravel is the head-chakra, which releases the white drop held there. As this drop descends in the central channel towards the heart, the dying person experiences an inner vision of a vast space filled with white light and this is called the 'mind of white appearance'. This drop then comes to rest in the heart-chakra, covering the indestructible drop of Clear Light from the top.

Next, the navel-chakra unravels and releases the red drop held there which slowly moves up the central channel towards the heart-chakra and the dying person has an inner vision of a vast space pervaded by red light, and this is called the 'mind of red-increase'. As these two drops converge at the heart-chakra, they completely enclose the Clear-Light drop and the dying person experiences black-darkness, all mindfulness ceases and one enters a deep swoon. Then the two drops separate and keep moving in opposite directions—the red drop moves up through the central channel and exits from the right nostril, and the white drop moves down and exits from the sexual organ.

During this period, while the drops are moving, the dying person experiences the Clear-Light Mind of death which is described as a vast, centre-less, limitless, lucid space that is crystal clear and devoid of any colour. If one is a skilful meditator, who has cultivated single-pointed meditation on the Clear Light while alive, one will now recognize the dawning of this all-pervasive mind and use it to cognize the emptiness of all phenomena. At that time, one will have a direct path to the Dharmakaya and the meditator's practice will be very profound. However, for others, the experience of the Clear Light will last according to one's karma; for some lasting for a few hours or days, and for others lasting for only a few moments.

THE INTERMEDIATE STATE (Sanskrit: *Antarabhava*)

For however long the Clear Light of Death may last, eventually, due to our instinctive grasping at a tangible world, the very subtle wind-energy of the Clear-Light Mind will stir. Carrying the karmic imprints from the previous life, it will again give rise to the grosser wind-minds in a process which is the reverse of that preceding death. From the Clear Light one will enter the black mind, the red mind, the white mind, and so on down to the mirage-like appearance. Then, instantly, one will arise in a ghostly, insubstantial intermediate body, similar to a dream-body.

Such a body will have its limbs and senses complete even if one were handicapped while alive. It will have a mind 'nine-times clearer' and sharper than when one was alive; and it will be able to pass through solid walls, mountains and arrive instantly wherever one wishes. Arising in such a body, the dead person will be able to see his or her corpse and one's mourning friends and relatives as if in a dream, but they will be unable to perceive him/her.

Depending on how attached one was to one's previous life-situation, one will suffer intensely 'like a fish on hot sand'. Some people, because of intense attachment, are even reborn as ghosts at this point, and then they haunt the person, place or thing to which they were attached. Some people even try to re-enter the corpse, but because the karma for that life is over, they are unable to do so and suffer intensely. At this point, dream-like visions begin to arise in the mind of the intermediate-state being, which depend largely on the kind of life one has just exited from. Virtuous people could see angels or saints or deities, depending on their belief system; Tantric meditators, familiar with the deities of a Tantric Mandala, could see the appearance of those deities; and evil, non-virtuous persons will see horrific nightmares of being persued by demons, armies and animals. Compelled by these visions, they will be forced to take rebirth in hell or as animals or in miserable human conditions.

If one is to be reborn as a human being, one will perceive signs concerning the continent and region where one is going to be reborn. One will also see other intermediate state beings who are going to be reborn in similar conditions and one can be seen by clairvoyant yogis. Eventually, driven by karma, one will arrive at the place where one's future parents are copulating. Seeing them clearly, and driven by gut instinct, one will feel lust for the parent of the opposite sex and envy and hatred for the parent of the same sex. Trying to intervene in their copulation, one will perceive only the sexual organ of the parent of the opposite sex and feel anger and frustration at being unable to unite with that parent.

The intermediate state being will then 'die', absorbing inwards into the drop of Clear Light in a process similar to the one described earlier. This drop of Clear Light will then be drawn, as if in a vortex, into the father's central channel and, at the moment of orgasm, will be emitted into the mother's womb 'riding on the horse of semen'. There, fertilizing the mother's ovum, it will be enclosed within the two white and red drops of one's parent 'like a diamond in an amulet box'. And this composite entity, which consists of the Clear-Light Mind and its wind-energy plus the red and white material drops from one's parents, will then develop into the psychophysical complex which will be the basis of designation of a new person in a new life.

It should be evident that Buddhists reject the materialist hypothesis that immaterial consciousness can arise from gross mind-less matter. Moments of consciousness can arise only from like causes, thus, the principal cause of each moment of consciousness is a previous moment of consciousness. Material entities like nervous systems and brains can only function as secondary supportive conditions to the primary cause, much as warmth and moisture act as the secondary supportive conditions in the growth of a seedling from its primary cause which is a seed.

Therefore, since each moment of consciousness must have a previous moment of consciousness as its primary cause, the Buddhists establish a beginningless continuum (Sanskrit: *Samtaan*) of the consciousness of each person. This stretches back to conception and beyond in a beginningless series of past lives, where the gross levels of sensory consciousness function in dependence on the secondary supportive condition of brain and nervous system, but arise from subtler levels of consciousness. These, in turn, arise from the subtle Fundamental Innate Mind of Clear Light.

Whereas the continuum of the grosser levels of mind is temporary, in that they arise and re-absorb back into their subtle source in ceaseless cycles, the continuum of the Clear-Light Mind is constant and everlasting, remaining as such from life to life. It is this Clear-Light Mind, our actual Buddha Nature, which, if left untended, keeps us tightly bound in the iron chains of our karma, life after life, but if carefully tended, this very Clear-Light Mind and its wind-energy become the Dharmakaya and Rupakaya of a Perfectly Enlightened Buddha.

REBIRTH

With one's primordial Clear-Light Mind trapped, as it were, by the red and white drops of one's parents forming the indestructible drop at the heart-chakra, the re-formation of the subtle energy system comprising the channels, drops and winds will recommence. First, the blue central channel will extend upwards and downwards from the indestructible drop, forming the 'axis of non-duality' of the whole energy system. Then, the white and red (sun and moon) channels of dual subject and object will differentiate and coil around the central channel, constricting it, and causing it to emanate out into the spokes of the chakras. A portion of the white drop will be held in the head-chakra as the 'male pole' of one's psychophysical organism, and a portion of the red drop will be held in the navel-chakra, forming the 'female pole'.

The channels and chakras will divide and subdivide until

the 72,000 channels of a human are complete. By now the physical organs are complete, and after a period of about ten months, the 'down-ward-voiding wind' of the mother will turn the foetus around and propel it through the birth canal. There the foetus will feel as if ground in a meat-grinder, and will re-emerge into the gross sensory world, screaming with shock and pain as the sense organs forcefully re-connect with their respective objects. The sights, sounds, smells, and sensations will come surging back to overwhelm the mind. A similar process occurs during the daily deep-sleep-dreaming-waking cycle but in a partial and reversible way.

RECOGNIZING ONE'S OWN BUDDHA POTENTIAL

By contemplating the above process, not only does the Tantric practitioner deepen one's conviction in the Buddhist doctrine of rebirth and karma but one also arrives at a definitive understanding of the profound Buddha Nature (*Tathagata garbha*) which the Buddha taught in the Sutras. The Sutras describe it as the negative quality of the emptiness of the mind, which allows for its transformation from the state of ignorance to the state of Enlightenment.

In the Highest Tantras, this Buddha Nature is specifically identified as the presence of a seminal drop of the subtlest mind of Clear Light and its wind-energy at the centre of the heart-chakra of all beings. Not only are all beings equal in this respect but they are also equal to the Buddhas because this Clear-Light Mind and its wind-energy are the final basis of designation of each and every person, including the Buddhas. As the *Hevajra Tantra* says,

> Just these Sentient Beings are Buddhas, but they are defiled by temporary stains. When those are removed, they are Buddhas.

The presence of the Clear Light wind-mind as our Buddha Nature, within the gross physical body-mind, is exemplified in the texts as the presence of a precious jewel in a muddy swamp, or gold in ore. As the famous mantra of Arya Avalokiteshwara says—OM MANI PADME HUM (OM jewel, in lotus HUM)—meaning the presence of the jewel of the Clear Light in the lotus (chakra) of the heart (the mantra has many other meanings also). In this way, the Tantric meditator recognizes that the basic material for the attainment of the enlightened state is within oneself, and that one does not have to go elsewhere to seek it.

The presence of the three states of waking-dreaming-deep sleep in our immediate experience are taken as examples (and proof) of the presence of the three deeper states of death-intermediate state-rebirth. These, in turn, are taken as examples (and proof) of the potential presence of the Three Bodies (or Two Bodies, if one takes the Sambhogakaya and Nirmanakaya together as the Rupakaya). This presence is identified specifically with the Clear Light wind-mind. The Clear-Light Mind being the potential Dharmakaya, and its wind-energy the potential Rupakaya.

According to Tantra, in order to realize the ultimate true nature of this world, one doesn't need billion-dollar particle accelerators, nuclear reactors, radio telescopes or electron microscopes. A simple, solitary, silent cave, high in the mountains, is sufficient. As one of my teachers, the very Venerable Gen Lamrimpa, says that if the scientists are really serious about understanding the nature of reality, they should generate the all-encompassing mind of Bodhichitta and Emptiness and practise Tantra!

FULFILLING THE BODHISATTVA VOW

Prior to entering a Tantric Mandala during initiation, it is mandatory to take the Bodhisattva vow in accordance with the Mahayana tradition. Thus, one would have to be a Mahayanist by motivation in order to practise the stages of Tantra. The basic Mahayana motivation is to work ceaselessly to overcome the two innate cognitive obstructions of the mind that prevent it from attaining Complete Enlightenment and the ability to truly benefit others.

The two obstructions are identified in Sutra as the Emotional Obstruction of the Delusions (Sanskrit: *Kleshavarana*), which prevent liberation from cyclic existence, and the deeper Cognitive Obstruction to Omniscience (Sanskrit: *Gye-avarana*) which prevents the mind from cognizing the Two Truths simultaneously. The Mahayana Bodhisattva vows to surmount these obstructions by practising the path of the Six Perfections of Generosity (Paramitayana) over three countless aeons of Time.

The Tantric Bodhisattva realizes that although the Paramitayana has been taught as a path to Enlightenment to encourage those for whom it is appropriate, it does not actually have the techniques to generate the Omniscient Dharmakaya and the Immortal Rupakaya. In Sutra, there are no techniques to generate the Clear-Light Mind, which is the only mind subtle enough to cognize the Two Truths simultaneously. Similarly, there are no concordant techniques to attain the 'Resident and Residence Mandalas' of the immortal Rupakaya. Therefore, in Sutrayana, there is actually no method to do so. Due to intense compassion for others and a keen intellect, the Tantric Bodhisattva would understand this deficiency of the Sutras and seek out the Tantric Path.

In Highest Tantras can be found the actual techniques of the Two Stages—the Generation and Completion Stages of Highest Secret Mantra—that transmute the iron chain of compulsive death-intermediate state-rebirth into the gold of the Three Bodies of a Buddha. This is done by transmuting the Clear-Light Mind into the omniscient, greatly blissful Dharmakaya, which is for one's own ultimate benefit, and by transmuting the wind-energy into the myriad Rupakaya which is for the ultimate benefit of others. A highly motivated Mahayanist would find in Tantra the means to fulfil the Bodhisattva vow that one has taken during entry into the Mahayana. This path is spoken of as being 'joyful in the beginning, joyful in the middle, and joyful in the end'.

By receiving the Four Initiations of Highest Yoga Tantra from a qualified Vajra Dhara Guru, the Clear-Light Mind and its wind-energy would be activated from 'within'. One would receive permission to use the resources of the world in general, and the particular 'raw material' of the waking-dreaming-deep sleep cycle and the faculty of sexual bliss, to reach the Clear Light within. It is said that when the right disciple meets the right Guru so that the Guru can work from 'within' while the disciple works from 'without', the progress of the disciple is as rapid as that of a boulder cast from a cliff.

◙

Buddha Vajradhara and consort

4. The Tantric Guru

'*Namo Guru Vajradhara.*
Worshipfully I prostrate at the lotus feet
of the Primordial Protector,
In the state of Union,
Who, from the pure space of Bliss-Emptiness,
Reveals the dance of the rainbow
Of the supremely magnificent Illusory Body,
Marked with the major and minor signs of perfection.'
—Yangchen Galo (eighteenth century)

THE VAJRADHARA GURU

THE TANTRIC GURU is the root of all Tantric attainments.
Without a guru who is a living, lineage-holder of the
unbroken chain of oral transmission traceable to the Buddha
himself, it is not possible to receive the requisite blessings,
initiations and crucial oral instructions. Without these, it is
not possible to even understand, let alone practise, the
extremely subtle and difficult yogas taught in the Tantric
texts. Furthermore, these texts and their commentaries are
often written in a coded 'Twilight Language' (Sanskrit:
Sandhya Bhasha) where euphemistic terms are used. Often,
one word or expression has various shades of meanings: the

superficial meaning, the inner context and a secret connotation. Moreover, what is conveyed by a living guru verbally or through facial expressions and gestures cannot be written down, but must be received in face-to-face encounters with the guru. The movements and expressions of the guru are considered to have great personal and symbolic significance for the disciple.

In the Tantras, it is stated that the original source of all the Tantras and Tantric Mandalas (systems) is Buddha Vajradhara (holder of the Vajra, or Indestructible Reality). He is the common Tantric symbolic form assumed by all the Buddhas of the past, present and future. This very subtle form is the basic Sambhogakaya. It is the centre and source of all the Tantric Mandalas which effortlessly emanate from and are withdrawn by this form in order to guide high beings like the Eighth to the Tenth Ground Bodhisattvas, high gods like Brahma and Ishwar, and human Tantric yogis.

Buddha Vajradhara is said to abide continuously in a special paradise of the highest Form Realm called Akanishta (Highest), in ceaseless union with his consort, the female Buddha Vajradhateshwari. Their perfect bodies are deep space-blue in colour and they wear the dazzling ornaments and robes of divine royalty. They and their world are completely insubstantial; the radiance of the Ultimate Clear Light symbolically expresses itself in this form.

Vajradhara, in his other manifestations, is also called Vajrasattva, the Primordial Heroic Being, and Adi Buddha, the Primordial Buddha. When elaborated further, this basic form appears as the fundamental Mandala of the Five Tathagatas and their elemental consorts and retinues. And when elaborated even further, they appear as the countless male and female, wrathful and peaceful deities of all the Tantric Mandalas, such as Heruka (to the senses of Bhairava), Kalachakra (to the senses of Kama Deva and Rudra) and Yamantaka (to the senses of Yama). Since these Sambhogakaya mandalas cannot be directly cognized by human disciples, the Buddha Vajradhara appears in the human realm in the Nirmanakaya form of the Tantric Guru, whom we can apprehend and relate to. Through the device of the Four Initiations and oral instructions, the guru helps us to first visualize and then directly cognize these Mandalas. The Tantric Guru is the disciple's sole means to access the Sambhogakaya, which is the only means for accessing the Dharmakaya. In this way, the disciple perceives the guru as a living embodiment of the Three Bodies of a fully Enlightened Buddha.

In the profound visualizations of Guru Yoga, which is the essence of Tantric practice, the disciple sees the guru in human form with Buddha Vajradhara and consort, haloed in rainbow-light, at the Guru's heart-chakra, and with a tiny blue HUNG-syllable at the heart of the divine couple. The HUNG-syllable, which symbolizes the Dharmakaya, emanates out as the Sambhogakaya form of Vajradhara and consort which emanate out as the physical form of the Tantric Master which is the Nirmanakaya. The guru is thus perceived by the disciple as a 'triple-being', simultaneously existing on three planes, of which only the physical one is evident to the senses of the disciple. It is crucial that the disciple learns to perceive the guru in this non-ordinary manner so that one is able to access the deeper levels of reality spanned by the guru.

Thus, a fully qualified Tantric Guru would be someone who has practised the whole Tantric Path to completion and has attained the resultant Three Bodies of a Buddha Vajradhara. At the least, a Tantric Guru should be someone who is a lineage-holder and whose level of realization is higher than one's own, who upholds the various levels of vows purely, and who is able to confer all the Tantric initiations flawlessly after having done the prerequisite retreats and mantra recitations.

It is said that a Tantric Guru is not someone whom one meets for the first time, but is one who has guided us in former lives and brought us to the present situation where we can again encounter the guru in accordance with our karma. In other words, the status, the level and external appearance of a guru and the kind of interaction one has with him/her is the result of one's own karma. Thus, the same guru can appear as being extremely kind to one disciple, while striking terror in the heart of another.

The qualities of such a master, and how to correctly relate to him/her, are taught in detail in a standard text called *Fifty Verses on the Spiritual Master* (Sanskrit: *Guru Panchashika*)[1] by the first century B.C. Indian Master, Arya Shura (also known as Ashvaghosh and Matichitta). The disciple is required to study and comprehend this text before entering into a Guru-disciple relationship. Normally, on encountering one's guru of this life, there is a period of probation during which the guru helps the disciple to stabilize in a correct relationship so that the maximum benefit can accrue to the disciple.

During this period, the Guru may seemingly 'test' the disciple by giving him/her apparently meaningless or difficult tasks. This is done to purify or to remove a karmic or mental block of a disciple that would later cause difficulties for the practitioner. As in the case of the famous Tibetan yogi Jetsun

Mila-Repa, whose guru, Lama Marpa, made him build, single-handedly, a double-storey house for his son, often asking him to break and remake it. When it was completed, the Master expressed his utter dislike of it and ordered Mila-Repa to tear it down and replace the mud and stones back from where he had brought them! Before coming to Lama Marpa, Mila-Repa had learnt sorcery and black magic with which he had devastated his enemies, killing several people and livestock, and destroying houses and fields. The serious seeker is advised to study the sacred biographies of past Indian and Tibetan masters and yogis in order to understand the subtle nuances of a Guru-disciple relationship.

The Tantric Guru-disciple relationship is the deepest possible one between two beings. Deeper even than all worldly relationships, including those with one's parents, family and community. Such a relationship cannot be artificial, contrived or superficial but is spontaneous and based on karmic instincts and a thorough comprehension of the doctrine so that the disciple understands what a Tantric Guru actually is. The relationship is not merely intellectual or academic but could span the entire personality of the disciple, from intellectual to emotional. From a true guru, nothing is hidden, no matter how much one may try to hide it, and since the goal is ultimate perfection of mind and body, the authentic Tantric Guru is unlikely to spare his disciple.

The disciple's unshakeable, reasoned belief in the truth of the Dharma manifests itself in a deep inner commitment to change and a desire to transform oneself in accordance with the path. And this is visible externally in a complete commitment to the guru.

A teacher become's one's Root Tantric Guru (Sanskrit:

Mula Guru) when one has formally received the complete set of the Four Initiations of Highest Tantra from him/her. During a preliminary ritual to the Four Initiations, in a profound 'ceremony', one 'dies' and is reborn as the divine child of the guru who is imagined in the divine form of the Tantric Deity. Until then, it is possible to transgress the teacher's word or even leave the teacher without incurring any fault, but once the Four Initiations have been received, there are grave karmic consequences if one transgresses the guru's word or dishonours or disrespects him/her in any way, even in one's dreams. Since the guru is going to deal with the deepest 'hidden' and 'secret' aspects of your personality, complete confidence and commitment are necessary for the disciple.

For people coming from cultures where words like 'reverence' and 'veneration' have no meaning, i.e. where one has not seen one's elders or peers 'venerating' or 'revering' anything, relating to a Tantric master would be very difficult, if not impossible. Also, since in such a relationship, a fake guru could easily exploit the gullible, great care must be taken to examine the antecedents and qualities of a Tantric Guru before one commits oneself. However, for a karmically destined relationship, the disciple (and also the guru) would have definite signs in the form of dreams, visions and omens to indicate the correctness of the relationship, as in the case of Naropa and Tilopa, and Mila-Repa and Marpa.

Having met such an authentic guru in accordance with one's karma, one should venerate the guru even in one's dreams, not daring to step over even his/her shadow. One should serve such a guru with whatever means one has, including material offerings, service and, above all, by intelligently following and accomplishing the guru's instructions and commands. In texts exemplifying how one should behave towards one's guru, the examples given are those of a devoted son to his father, a devoted woman to her husband, and a warrior to his liege lord.

THE PRELIMINARIES

Nowadays, the standard procedure is for the disciple to do the various sets of '1,00,000' preliminaries, prior to receiving the Four Initiations of Highest Yoga Tantra (sometimes they can be done immediately after receiving the initiations). There are four standard preliminaries, followed by all the four Tibetan orders, although each has its own variation and the preliminary practices vary in number: some have less while others have more. The four standard preliminaries are:

1. 1,00,000 visualizations of Guru Yoga.
2. 1,00,000 recitations and visualization of the 100-syllable Sanskrit mantra of Vajrasattva.
3. 1,00,000 full-length prostrations, with accompanying visualizations and recitation.
4. 1,00,000 Mandala offerings.

In addition to these, different lineages and gurus may require a disciple to complete other preliminaries like 1,00,000 offerings of water-bowls, 1,00,000 offerings of butter-lamps, making of 1,00,000 stamped clay images called *tsa-tsa* and 1,00,000 fire-offerings. A brief description of the four main preliminaries is given below:

(1) GURU YOGA

'This body of mine and your pure form, O Guru,
This mantra of mine and your pure speech, O Guru,

> *This mind of mine and your pure heart, O Guru,*
> *By your blessing transform my three doors*
> *To become inseparably one with yours.'*
> —Mahamudra prayer to the gurus

Guru Yoga is the foundation of the Tantric Sadhana (a formal Tantric meditation session). Although it is the foremost of the preliminaries, it is the basic foundation for the more complex visualizations and practices of the Generation and Completion Stages of Highest Yoga Tantra.

Each Tantra has its own specific Guru Yoga, associated with the deity and Mandala of that particular Tantra. In general, the practitioner, while sitting in formal meditation sessions, single-pointedly visualizes the guru in the form of Buddha Vajradhara or one's Tantric deity called 'Yidam' in Tibetan (Sanskrit: *Ishta-devata*), which is the span of one's hand in size, on the crown of one's head.[2] After reciting the prayer, one requests the guru to descend and bless one's 'Three doors of action'—body, speech and mind—so that they 'merge' with those of the guru and thereby be transformed into the Three Kayas of Enlightened action—the body into the Nirmanakaya, speech into the Sambhogakaya, and mind into the Dharmakaya.

The guru's form then becomes smaller (about thumb-size), and descends through the 'Brahma-randra' (fontanelle aperture at the crown of the head) into the Blue Central Channel of the disciple. Descending to the head-chakra, the guru emits white light and blesses the white drop located there. The white drop is said to be the basis of the perception of form, including one's own body, and the sights, sounds, smells, tastes and tactile objects which form the continuum of the waking state.[3] The drop, which for ordinary beings perceives the impure appearance of the world, when blessed like this, attains the capacity to cognize the pure appearances of the Enlightened mind.

The Guru Vajradhara then descends into the throat-chakra and emits a red light that blesses the red drop located there, which is responsible for impure speech and for impure appearances in dreams, transforming it to perceive the Sambhogakaya and thereby to communicate pure Dharma to all beings at all levels. Descending from there, the Vajradhara Guru arrives at the heart-chakra and emitting blue light blesses the 'indestructible drop' of Clear Light located there, which is responsible for consciousness and for the impure blank state of deep sleep, transforming it so as to develop its capacity to apprehend the formless Dharmakaya. Growing smaller and smaller in size, the Vajradhara Guru absorbs into the 'indestructible drop', thereby 'taking possession' of one's subtlest basis of designation.

This is a profound yoga whose benefits can only be understood by a practitioner. Apart from aiding the disciple's initial familiarization with the pathways of the channels and chakras, at the least, it helps in decreasing the psychological distance between the disciple and the guru.

The above visualizations need to be done 1,00,000 times along with a recitation of the deity's mantra and/or the guru's 'Name-mantra'.

(2) THE VAJRASATTVA MANTRA

The recitation of the 100 syllable Vajrasattva Mantra, along with its corresponding visualization, is an essential Tantric practice meant to purify past negative karma and to restore broken Tantric pledges and commitments (Sanskrit:

Samaya). Therefore, this is not just a preliminary practice, but an essential part of the later sadhana practice, like the Guru Yoga. It is essential for the practitioner to become intimately familiar with it.

If one has not yet received the four empowerments of Highest Yoga Tantra, one should visualize Vajrasattva alone. If one has received such empowerments, it is mandatory to visualize Vajrasattva in union with his consort, Vajra Prabhavati. In the latter case, it leads to the initial purification of the trainee's sexual faculty through visualizing it in a pure context, free of all negative associations. The sexual union of the deities symbolizes the greatly blissful and pure nature of the continuum of the Primordially Enlightened Mind, which is the non-dual basis of reality, and is completely realized by one's guru and yet to be realized by oneself.

In the visualization one sees one's guru in the aspect of Vajrasattva, at the crown of one's head, radiant and in the dazzling white colour of a snow-mountain struck by sunlight. To this manifestation of the guru, the disciple remorsefully confesses any wrongdoing or broken Samaya, pledges not to transgress again, and seeks the inspiration of the guru to help protect oneself in future. Then one requests the Guru to purify oneself of the negative karma that one has accumulated, which is imagined as being present in one's body as black fluid, or as scorpions and snakes!

One imagines that the Guru Vajrasattva grants one's request, and as one recites the 100-syllable mantra, cleansing nectars, white in colour, flow down from the guru's body into one's own through the fontanelle and eliminate the black fluid or scorpions through one's lower body, thereby purifying one's body. Visualization and recitation of the mantra is repeated 1,00,000 times or till definite signs of purification appear in one's dreams. One could dream of eliminating black fluids or scorpions from one's body, or of vomiting, or bathing and washing, maybe with milk or light. It is advisable to continue such a practice until these signs appear.

There are many variations of this visualization in different lineages, such as the impurities being purified immediately, or exiting as black smoke from the pores of one's body. One could also visualize the syllables of the mantra revolving in a rosary of light around the seed syllable HUNG at the Guru-Deity's heart as one recites the mantra.

OM VAJRASATTVA SAMAYA MANUPALAYA VAJRASATTVA TVENO PRATISHTHA DHRDHO ME BHAV SUTUSHYO ME BHAV SUPASHYO ME BHAV ANURAKTO ME BHAV SARVA SIDDHI ME PRAYACCHA SARVA KARMA SUCHA ME CHITTAM SHRIYAM KURU HUM HA HA HA HA HOH BHAGVAN VAJRASATTVA SARVA TATHAGATA VAJRA MA ME MUNCHA VAJRI BHAV MAHA SAMAYA SATTVA AH HUM PHAT.

(3) PROSTRATIONS

Again, this is an important purification practice, which also accumulates merit. It helps to promote a more humble disposition in the proud and arrogant. As a preliminary practice prior to fully engaging with a Tantric Guru, it is indispensable for this very reason. To approach a Tantric Guru with arrogance because of race, social status, wealth, caste, or academic qualifications is a sure way to block the flow of the guru's grace and wisdom. As in the case of Jetsun Mila-Repa who came to his Guru, acutely conscious of being a skilled sorcerer. As a result, his Guru assigned him the lowest manual labour, treated him harshly, and sarcastically referred to him as 'The Great Magician'. Then, Mahasiddha Naropa, who prided himself on his intellectual prowess, scholarly accumen and purity as a monk, had the onerous task of dealing with his guru, the Mahasiddha Tilopa, who appeared to him in the form of a dirty, drunken, foul-mouthed beggar, who put Naropa through severe humiliation in order to cure him. So, if one's Guru merely asks one to do 1,00,000 prostrations, he is being very kind indeed.

In this practice, one visualizes the Thirty-Five Confession Buddhas[4] surrounding one's guru in the centre, who appears in the aspect of Buddha Shakyamuni. Confessing all wrongdoing, one pays homage to each of the Buddhas by reciting their name and prostrating by touching one's folded hands to the crown of one's head, to one's throat, and to one's heart and then lying full length on the ground and stretching one's arms out in front. One then immediately stands up and repeats the process for each of the Thirty-Five Buddhas. One goes on repeating this in a batch of thirty-five, over and over again, counting with beads as one goes along. Since one is prostrating with one's body, chanting with one's mouth, and visualizing the Thirty-Five Buddhas with one's mind, one is engaging all three 'doors' of action, thereby purifying them of their negative karma, while, simultaneously, accumulating merit through prostrating to a Buddha-form. Again, the beneficial effects of this exercise can be understood only by someone who has done it. It is said that reciting the names of the Thirty-Five Confession Buddhas can purify negativity of body, speech and mind because of specific vows made by those Buddhas while they were Bodhisattvas practising the path.

(4) MANDALA OFFERING

This is primarily a merit-generating activity, in which one offers the whole world-system to the Guru with all desirable things in it. This pure world, imagined in accordance with the classical Indian description, is said to consist of a central axis which protrudes out of the earth as the mythical Mount Meru (which some say is Mount Kailash on the Indo-Tibetan border). Surrounding this axis is a vast ocean and in it are four major continents called Jambudwipa in the south (which is the Indo-Asian continent), Uttara Kuru in the north, Purva Videha in the east, and Apar Godaniya in the west. Each continent has two subcontinents near it.

One uses an external symbolic representation of this Mandala, using a base as a plate. In its centre, one makes a small heap symbolizing Mt Meru, around it one makes four smaller heaps and eight smaller heaps, representing the continents and their subcontinents. One then removes the heaps with one's hands, and repeats the process again and again. One should use material according to one's wealth, such as a base of gold and heaps of jewels. But one can use anything, including sand and stones. While doing this, one repeats the standard libation prayer, describing the world and the offerings. Again, one uses one's mind to visualize a pure world, one's speech to recite the liturgy, and one's body to construct the physical mandala, in this way accumulating merit.

Having received permission from one's guru to carry out the preliminaries, it is best to do them continuously by devoting all one's time and energy to them in retreat. One can do the preliminaries serially or by mixing them, and if one spends all one's waking time doing them, they can take up to a year or two to accomplish. The power of these practices should not be underestimated. If done correctly and with concentration, they purify any negative karma or mental block that can arise as a serious obstacle as one goes deeper into the practice. As mentioned earlier, definite signs of purification occur in one's dreams.

The Vajrasattva practice is specially beneficial and powerful and can be used for self-healing when one is afflicted with physical problems due to broken samaya. Not only do these practices act as a purificatory ritual, but because of their repetitive nature, they also set the foundation for the daily Tantric Sadhana, which when performed intensively in solitary retreat is done four to six times a day, daily, without break. Only by such painstaking repetitive practice, done in a concerted manner over long periods of time, can progress be made on this extremely difficult meditative path. Also, these practices serve to break the habitual thought patterns and routines that bind one to an ordinary, ignorant way of life.

TANTRIC INITIATION

An aspiring Tantric practitioner becomes a fit vessel for initiation after one has, first, taken refuge from the depths of one's heart in the Three Precious Jewels of the Buddha, the Dharma and the Sangha, and in particular in one's guru as the personification of these three objects of refuge. Secondly, through studying the tenets of the Hinayana, such as the Four Noble Truths and the Bhava Chakra, one should have gained a clear comprehension of the deepest level of suffering, its origin, and the means to terminate it, so that one feels a constant wish to free oneself from cyclic existence.

Thirdly, through studying the tenets of the Mahayana,

a practitioner should have a deep desire to enter the path of the Bodhisattvas who aspire to the Complete Enlightenment of a Buddha. This wish should be based on a mind of 'Great Compassion', which is generated through effort by practising such teachings as the 'Mind Transformation' (*Lo-Jong*) teachings of the Kadampa Geshes of Tibet. Fourthly, and most important, one should have reached the level of 'inferential Cognition' of Emptiness as it is defined in the Prasangika Madhyamika System of Acharya Chandrakirti. At the least, one should have a view of the 'lower' Mahayana philosophical school of 'Chittamatra' (Mind-only) in order to begin Tantric practice, but, eventually, one must understand Emptiness as it is taught in the higher Prasangika system.

At best, one should have actual experience of these four prerequisites, and, at the least, one should have an unmistaken conceptual comprehension of them. Then, having found a fully qualified Tantric Guru towards whom one feels genuine devotion, and having done the 'hundred thousand' preliminary practices under his/her advice and guidance, one is now ready to 'enter the ocean of Tantra'. In this, the role of the living Tantric Guru is crucial as it is through his/her kindness that one enters and becomes part of the living lineage of oral transmission and blessing. These can only flow through living masters, and are deemed so precious that gurus communicate them verbally to their disciples, generation after generation, traceable back to the Buddha Shakyamuni and his spiritual descendants.

THE THREE 'LOWER' TANTRA LEVELS

As in the Sutras, the Buddha has taught the Tantras in a sequential manner. For beginners, whose powers of visualization are not yet fully developed, the Buddha has taught simple Sadhanas, which increase in complexity and scope as one progresses higher in the Tantra levels. In the various levels of Tantra, it is essential to have reached an inferential cognition of Emptiness as it is taught in the Prasangika Madhyamika system of the Sutras. It is in this 'inner space' of Emptiness that the practitioner cancels out all ordinary appearance of 'self and other' and, instead, visualizes in vivid three-dimensional detail, like a hologram projected by the mind, a perfect reality embodied as a divine being in a divine world.

The purpose of the visualization is to block and negate our habitual sense of 'ordinariness' about ourselves and our world, and to prepare the mind to cognize reality as it actually is—i.e. primordially perfect and pure. This is one of the principal purposes of Tantra. With this aim in mind, the Tantras are divided into four sets:

(1) Kriya (action) Tantra;
(2) Charya (behaviour) Tantra;
(3) Yoga Tantra;
(4) Maha-anuttara Yoga Tantra (Highest Yoga Tantra) (Maha Guhya Mantra).

These divisions are also made in terms of the practitioner's ability to sustain sexual bliss and to use that blissful awareness to meditate on Emptiness.

1. KRIYA TANTRA: In Kriya Tantra, great emphasis is placed on austere external actions such as ritual, ablutions and on creating a pure and clean environment. Strict vegetarianism, fasting, along with recitation of mantra are practised to invoke the Ultimate Reality as a physically manifest deity

to whom one relates as a servant does to a master.

A typical sadhana of the Kriya Tantra level would involve the following procedure. Having received the *Jenang* (permission) of a particular deity, such as the white pacific form of Arya Tara or Arya Avalokiteshwara (both of whom are Buddhas manifesting in the form of eighth-ground Bodhisattvas), the practitioner would set up a clean place. The place earmarked for meditation would be smeared with cow dung and other products regarded as being pure. The practitioner would follow the eight Mahayana precepts of: (1) not to kill (even a mosquito); (2) not to steal; (3) to be celibate (which means avoiding even self-stimulation); (4) to speak no lies; (5) to desist from intoxicants; (6) to take only one meal in the twenty-four hour period; (7) not to sit on high ornate seats, thrones, beds, animal skins; (8) to wear no jewellery, perfume or any other adornments.

Having followed such an ascetic regimen, the practitioner, after washing, should sit on a specially prepared meditation seat and assume the seven-fold posture of Vairochana (the posture of the Buddha seated in meditation). He would then focus on Emptiness and invoke the appearance of the deity through a symbolic ritual hand-gesture, or seed-syllable, or mantra sound. In this way, the deity is visualized in detail in three dimensions, as the appearance–aspect of Emptiness, luminous and radiant. The 'servant-disciple' invokes the blessings of the deity through offerings, prayers and vows, absorbs the deity into himself and then absorbs his mind and speech in the recitation of the deity's mantra. Practising in this way, the yogi can attain the supernormal powers of a god of the Desire Realm.

The level of sexual bliss that the trainee of this level of Tantra is permitted to 'use as a path' is the bliss arising from male and female deities, looking or exchanging glances, without any physical contact.

2. CHARYA TANTRA: Also called Ubhaya Tantra, in this level of Tantra, the visualization of deities becomes more complex. Although one still engages in austere external activities such as ritual and fasting, there is greater emphasis on internal meditative stabilization. A practitioner would meditate on Emptiness and invoke the deity, such as Arya Manjushree, and relate to the deity on equal terms. A trainee of Charya Tantra would be able to sustain the bliss of male and female deities making preliminary physical contact, such as holding hands and smiling at each other.

3. YOGA TANTRA: In Yoga Tantra, the emphasis is mainly on internal meditative stabilization, as the complexity of the deities and their retinues and Mandalas (residence) becomes more complex. Also, wrathful forms such as the Bodhisattva Vajrapani become the objects of meditation. At this level, the trainee is able to 'metabolize' the bliss of male and female deities embracing.

4. HIGHEST YOGA TANTRA: At this profoundest level of inner yoga, all the deities are manifestly or symbolically in sexual union with their respective consorts. The trainee should initially be able to sustain the bliss of orgasm without emission during the 'generation stage'. Later, one should be able to sustain the 'Great Bliss' (Sanskrit: *Mahasukha*) that is many times greater than that of orgasm, and which arises exclusively as a result of the 'completion stage' practices when the mind-energies are brought into the central channel to abide and cease there.

In order to enter into the practices of Highest Yoga Tantra, which are the actual techniques that transform an ordinary human being into an omniscient, immortal Buddha, it is necessary to receive, in the right order, and without error, the Four Initiations that are mandatory to all the Highest Tantras. Sometimes, they are elaborated differently, as in the Kalachakra system, where there are eleven sets of initiations.

The Tantric Bodhisattva cultivates a practitioner's mind as carefully as a farmer does a field. The hard rocks of immorality and evil are first cleared with practices of the Hinayana, and then the soil is fertilized by the rich manure of 'Great Compassion' that is the heart of the Mahayana. Having first prepared the field of one's mind, one is now ready to receive into it the seeds of Tantra that will eventually ripen into the Trikaya of a fully Enlightened Buddha. Due to one's own good karma, diligently cultivated in past lives, the practitioner meets his/her destined Tantric Master, who casts these seeds into all three levels of one's mind—the gross, the subtle and the very subtle.

It is said in the texts that highly developed practitioners attain the 'Resultant State' through the process of initiation, whereas others attain realization and visions of what is to come. At the highest level, actual substances and consorts are used, whereas for beginners these are merely visualized through symbols. These initiations are always given 'into' a 'mandala' of a Tantric Deity. Again, for the highest level of practitioners, the guru actually emanates the whole Mandala in three-dimensions, with all the deities actually present, as in the case of the king Indrabodhi and his Guru Buddha Shakyamuni, or as in the case of Lama Marpa of Tibet and his Indian guru, the Mahasiddha Naropa. However, in standard public initiations nowadays, a painted cloth mandala (Tibetan: *Thanka*) or a coloured sand-particle mandala is used. A painting of the central deity (and consort) may also be used.

The initiations are normally given over a period of three days. During the first day, the disciples are reborn as the children of the Father-Mother central deity who is imagined to be the guru, who clears obstacles and hindrances, and gives the disciples sacred threads meant for protection and blades of auspicious Kusha grass.[5] These are placed under the pillow and mattress of the disciple during the initiation process in order to ward off evil omens and bad dreams.

The disciple is instructed to observe his/her dreams on the first night, where positive or negative 'omens' may appear concerning the disciple's future progress and relation to the Tantric deity. On the second day, the First 'Vase' Empowerment is conferred on the disciple, and on the third day, the other three empowerments are conferred. The whole ceremony concludes with the offering of a feast (Sanskrit: *Gana-chakra*).

THE FOUR INITIATIONS

Each of the Four Initiations introduces the disciple to progressively deeper levels of reality through symbolic means; the Fourth Initiation culminates in revealing the resultant state beyond symbols and expressions. Each initiation has many levels of meaning, and the full meaning of each becomes evident to the disciple only later through intensive cultivation of the practices associated with each initiation.

The Four Initiations are: (1) The Vase Initiation (Sanskrit: *Kalash-abhisheka*); (2) The Secret Initiation (Sanskrit: *Guhyabhisheka*); (3) The Transcendent-Wisdom Initiation

(Sanskrit: *Pragya-gyan-abhisheka*); (4) The Fourth Initiation (Sanskrit: *Chaturabhisheka*).

(1) THE VASE INITIATION: This is so called because it is conferred primarily through the waters of a vase and other symbolic substances. It is bestowed in a manner similar to the anointment of a king with authority to overcome evil and ensure the good of the land. Similarly, through this empowerment, the initiate is authorized to overcome 'ordinary appearances' through meditating on the Generation Stage of Highest Yoga Tantra. Specifically, one is qualified to visualize oneself as the deity of the Mandala, along with the consort, retinue and residence mandalas, and to recite the mantras, and engage in activities pleasing to those deities. Later, one is introduced to the 'Five Enlightened Families' of the 'Fundamental Mandala of the Five Tathagatas' and their respective consorts and retinues. And, finally, one is empowered as a 'Vajra Master', i.e. a Tantric Teacher empowered to initiate and teach others.

THE FUNDAMENTAL MANDALA OF THE FIVE TATHAGATAS

In the Sutras, the Buddha has taught that a person exists in dependence on his/her five aggregates (Sanskrit: *Panchaskandha*). First, the aggregate of 'form' (Sanskrit: *Rupa skandha*) which includes one's own body and all the sensory objects within one's own continuum, i.e. all the sights, sounds, odours, tastes and tactile sensations. Second, when this aggregate of form becomes fully active at birth, the various sense organs come into contact with their respective sense objects and there arises the second mental aggregate of 'feeling' (Sanskrit: *Vedana skandha*). Then, as feelings are experienced, the mind begins discriminating between pleasant, unpleasant and neutral sensory objects and between the individual characteristics of objects, and there arises the third aggregate of 'discrimination' (Sanskrit: *Sangya-skandh*). These discriminations are based on the fourth aggregate of 'prior conditioning' from former lives (Sanskrit: *Samskara-Skandha*) which are further reinforced or altered by one's actions. Finally, there arises the overall 'consciousness' aggregate (Sanskrit: *Vigyana-skandha*) of a being which comprises the five sense-consciousnesses and the sixth mental consciousness of concepts, ideas and thought.

When these five aggregates are fully operational and appear as the psychophysical 'whole', they are the basis of designation of 'I', 'me', 'him', 'her'. For all ordinary beings, these aggregates are necessarily the products of past ignorant karma (as outlined in the Bhava Chakra) and are therefore referred to as 'the contaminated aggregates'. It is these which are purified and transformed into the pure aggregates of a Buddha i.e. the pure basis of designation of a Buddha.

The five aggregates are transformed through the Tantric path into the Five Primordial Wisdoms of the Enlightened Mind, each personified as a Tathagata (Buddha), and the five elements associated with the aggregate of form are transformed into the Five Elemental Consorts of these Buddhas. In Tantric terms, it is said that the Fundamental Innate Mind of Clear Light has an intrinsic 'radiance' of five colours—white, red, blue, green and yellow. It is these five 'radiances' which, in the unenlightened stage, appear as the five contaminated aggregates, and the five gross mundane elements of earth, water, fire, air and space. In the mind, they appear as the five basic poisons (delusions) of ignorance, lust, anger, pride and jealousy. When the energy of these delusions, principally of ignorance, lust and anger is harnessed on the Tantric Path, then the five contaminated aggregates are transformed into the 'Lords of the Five Buddha Families'.

The aggregate of form is transformed into the 'Wisdom of the Expanse of Reality' (Sanskrit: *Dharmadhatv-Gyan*) which is embodied as the White Buddha Vairochana, lord of the 'Tathagata Family'. The aggregate of consciousness is purified and transformed into the 'mirror-like wisdom' (Sanskrit: *Adarshagyan*), which is embodied as the Blue Buddha Akshobhya, Lord of the 'Vajra Family'. The aggregate of feeling is transformed into the 'Wisdom of Discernment' (Sanskrit: *Pratyavekshana-gyan*), which is embodied as the Red Buddha Amitabha, lord of the 'Lotus Family'. The aggregate of discrimination is transformed into the 'Wisdom of Sameness' (Sanskrit: *Samatagyan*), embodied as the Yellow Buddha Ratna Sambhava, lord of the 'Jewel Family'. The aggregate of 'Karmic conditioning' is transformed into the 'Wisdom of Accomplishment' (Sanskrit: *Krtyanusthanagyan*), embodied as the Green Buddha Amoghasiddhi, lord of the 'Sword Family'.

The five elements of the aggregate of form are transformed into the five elemental consorts of the Five Buddhas. Space is transformed into the female Buddha, Akash-Dhateshwari, consort of the White Buddha Vairochana. Air (motility) is transformed into the female Buddha, Samaya Tara, consort of the Green Buddha Amoghasiddhi. Fire is transformed into the female Buddha Pandaravasini, consort of the Red Buddha Amitabha. Water is transformed into the female Buddha Lochana, consort of the Blue Buddha Akshobhya. Earth is transformed into the female Buddha Mamaki, consort of the Yellow Buddha

Ratna Sambhava.

When these five Buddha couples and their retinues are arrayed in 'inner space', Akshobhya Buddha and his consort Lochana occupy the centre,[6] with Amitabha Buddha and Pandaravasini in the west, Vairochana Buddha and Akash-Dhateshwari in the east, Amoghasiddhi Buddha and Samaya Tara in the north, Ratna Sambhava Buddha and Mamaki in the south, then such an arrangement is called the 'Fundamental Mandala of the Five Tathagatas'. It is the basis of designation of the fundamental Sambhogakaya of all the Buddhas, which is called Buddha Vajradhara and Buddha Vajradhateshwari, who form the 'Sixth Family' that subsumes the other five. All the deities of the Mandalas of Highest Yoga Tantra—peaceful, semi-wrathful or very wrathful—are further elaborations, or emanations, of these five fundamental Buddha couples, to teach and guide specific types of disciples.

Thus, in the Vase Initiation, the disciple is introduced to the potential presence of these 'Six' Buddha families within oneself, through their symbols and substances. The Vase Initiation activates the white drop in the head-chakra, which for common beings produces the ordinary appearances of the world, but is now empowered to produce the pure 'Vajra' appearances of the deity and its mandala. It also activates the potential of the disciple to attain the Nirmanakaya (emanation body) of flesh and blood that appear in human (and other) forms to guide sentient beings.

2. THE SECRET INITIATION: In this initiation, the blindfolded initiate offers a visualized consort as the basis of bliss to the Guru-Deity and, in return, receives the 'secret' male and female substances of the deity and consort, symbolized by a

mixture of white yoghurt and red jaggery (coarse sugar). On tasting these substances, the initiate imagines a corresponding state of bliss, and when this blissful awareness is focused on Emptiness, then the second Secret Initiation is received. It authorizes the disciple to engage in the Completion Stage practices associated with the channels, chakras, winds and drops and to eventually attain the Buddha's Sambhogakaya. The 'tasting' of the secret substances also activates the 'red-drop' at the throat-chakra, which for ordinary beings produces worldly speech, but is now empowered to produce pure 'Vajra' speech.

3. THE TRANSCENDENT-WISDOM INITIATION: In this initiation, the visualized consort offered to the guru-deity is returned to the disciple whose blindfold is removed. Visualizing oneself as the deity, the initiate enters into union with the consort. Due to the 'inner fire' of desire as the white drop in the head-chakra melts and is imagined to flow in the central channel in a controlled manner, the initiate imagines experiencing the exclusive 'Great Bliss' of the Completion Stage. When this blissful awareness meditates on Emptiness, one receives the Third Initiation which plants the seed to attain the Buddha's omniscient Dharmakaya.

The indestructible drop, containing the Fundamental Innate Mind of Clear Light enclosed in the red-white drops from one's parents at the heart-chakra, is activated and the disciple is empowered to attain the non-conceptual transcendent wisdom that characterizes the Dharmakaya of all the Buddhas.

4. THE FOURTH INITIATION: This initiation is simply called the 'Fourth' or 'Word' Initiation because in it the guru describes

to, and therefore empowers, the disciple to attain the resultant state of the Union (Sanskrit: *Yuga-naddha*) of the omniscient mind (Dharmakaya) with the omnipresent form (Rupakaya), which is called the Resultant Union of the Two Truths, attained at the end of the Completion Stage of Highest Yoga Tantra. All three drops at the head, throat and heart chakra are simultaneously activated so that the disciple attains the resultant Swabhavikakaya (Nature Body) that is the composite of the Three Bodies.

Further Instructions: The initiate who has received the four empowerments in the correct sequence without error, must then receive experiential guidance, step by step, from the guru. Normally, the guru will explain to the disciple the exact practice to be followed. The disciple will then apply the techniques taught by the guru in intensive meditative retreats, and then report back to the guru once the first step has been accomplished. The guru will then teach the rest of the steps, one by one, as each is accomplished. Although the general Tantric Path comprising the various divisions of the Generation and Completion Stages is the same for all the practitioners, the specific techniques and procedures to be followed vary from individual to individual. It is the guru's responsibility to choose the correct procedures from the vast array of methods taught in the different Tantras. It is the disciple's responsibility to put those methods into practise.

The ideal disciple should be like the Mahasiddha Luipada (sixth-seventh century A.D.), who, on receiving the initiations and 'further instructions' from his guru, was so intent on practising them that he decided he had no time to waste in trying to find comfortable environs. Coming upon a fishing village on the banks of the Ganges, he saw that the fishermen regularly gutted their catch on the beach before taking the fish to sell in the city. Deciding that it was sufficient, he found a secluded spot nearby and forgetting the world, practised intensely, surviving on the regular supply of fish offal. He attained Enlightenment in that very life. The great Yogi Mila-Repa, finding no other means to sustain himself, lived on a diet of nettle soup until his entire body turned green! He too attained perfect Enlightenment in that very life.

There is no greater fortune than to encounter this system and to have the leisure and means to practise it. The wise, therefore, abandon all else to devote their whole life to it.

🔲

5. The Tantric Path

*'Then, when you have properly understood
The essentials of the Three Principals of the Path,
Devote yourself to solitude, and by developing the power
of enthusiasm,
Fulfil your eternal longing, swiftly, my son!'*
          —Lama Tsongkhapa (fourteenth century A.D.)

THE NEED FOR SOLITUDE

ALTHOUGH FOR AN advanced Tantric meditator the solitude of a forest or cremation ground is identical to the 'solitude' in the centre of a busy marketplace, for beginners it is essential to resort to actual seclusion. A solitary place should ideally be one free of commotion and from the coming and going of people. Such a place is necessary not only to develop the essential focused mind of both Sutra and Tantra called Shamatha (calm-abiding), but also to help the mind overcome its habitual addiction to 'ordinariness' which is constantly reinforced through contact with 'ordinary' people, their institutions and systems.

Solitude is a dangerous place. It is what the world metes out as extreme punishment to criminals. If one's mind has not been matured by a deep experience of the Three Principals of the Path—renunciation, Bodhichitta and the correct view of Emptiness—in solitude, one's uncontrolled mind, cluttered with emotional baggage and wrong views, will

Lama Tsong-Khapa

tilt towards insanity. Therefore, even for one who has cultivated and controlled the mind through hearing, study and reflection, it is advisable to take solitude in measured doses, and to increase one's capacity for it as one goes along. This is best done in formal 'retreats' where one voluntarily fixes a time, say three months, where one resolves to give up all connection with the world and to focus one's mind 'inwards' through the techniques of Tantra.

Then, having made all necessary arrangements for provisions and essentials, one completely withdraws one's energy-investment from the world and reinvests it in formal, seated meditation. This was borne out by the great Yogi Mila-Repa who instructed his foremost disciple, the Venerable Rechungpa, about how vital seated meditation was, when they were finally parting. As Rechungpa walked away, Mila-Repa called out to him to receive his final instruction. As Rechungpa turned around reverently, Mila-Repa too turned around, bent over, and uncovered his buttocks, callused and hardened through years of seated meditation in rocky caves!

It is essential that, at the outset, the beginner understands that Tantric meditation is perhaps the most difficult task a human being can undertake, and that it requires great effort and perseverance applied over long periods of time. For this to happen, complete confidence in the guru, in the teaching, and in oneself are essential.

Deeply entrenched internal inertia, ignorance and delusion have to be overcome and nothing short of a warrior-like stance will accomplish this. Since even the intellectual comprehension of the path is difficult, to be able to hew out the gem of personal experience from the mountain of internal and external resistance is a formidable task worthy only of great 'heroes and heroines' (Sanskrit: *Vira* and *Virani*)—terms used in Tantric texts to refer to practitioners of the Tantric path. This is so because once the disciple has received the blessings, initiations and further instructions from one's lama, then it is one's own responsibility to carry them out flawlessly. This would mean living one's life in such a way so that the maximum time, effort and energy are devoted to the task of meditation.

Wisely recognizing the limits set by one's own karma, one must manoeuvre skilfully through the turmoil of life, avoiding all extremes, and setting the limits of the renunciant and a Bodhisattva to one's own conduct. One must curb one's devious and vagrant worldly mind, and tie it to the Yogas of the Two Stages of Highest Secret Mantra—The Generation and Completion Stages.

UTPANNAKRAM–THE GENERATION STAGE

The Generation Stage of Highest Secret Mantra is like the rehearsal for a play's final performance, in which the initiate's mind is enriched in both subtlety and creative vision. It functions as a bridge over the vast chasm separating an ordinary, limited being from the omniscient Buddha. This chasm is bridged by 'taking the result as the path' in which the meditator uses one's imagination to conceive a vision of the resultant state of Buddhahood as the attainment of the Three Kayas. This is called the 'imaginary' or 'illusion-like' yoga, because though one is definitely not yet a Buddha, one nevertheless uses one's understanding of the Emptiness and dependent-existence of all phenomena to cancel out the mundane, limited appearance of oneself and one's world, and to replace it in intense meditation with the vision of oneself as a Buddha in a perfect world.

One has been empowered by the guru to do this during the Vase Initiation ceremony in which one is shown the form of the Buddha-Deity, his/her retinue, and residence mandalas on which one should meditate during the Generation Stage. The philosophical basis behind this being that while in the Sutras, Emptiness is taught as the fundamental characteristic of the mundane, ordinary world perceived by ignorant beings, in Tantra, the Ultimate Reality of the Enlightened State is taught as a primordially indivisible coalescence of Emptiness and 'pure appearance'. Since phenomena do not exist independently of the consciousnesses that perceive them, but do exist dependent on designation by those consciousnesses, the Tantric meditator realizes that ignorant beings designate into existence an impure self ('I') that appears to their minds because of past karma based on ignorance, and that it need not be so.

So, by meditating on Emptiness, one mentally annuls the appearance of one's own 'impure' psychophysical aggregates, which are the basis of an 'ordinary' limited self ('I'). Instead, one visualizes a pure basis of designation which is the male-female divine form of the Buddha-deity, ornamented with thirty-two major and eighty minor signs of physical perfection, characteristic of a Buddha's form-body, as the basis of designation of an enlightened self ('I'). In this way, one 'shifts' the designated self (I) from an impure, ordinary, gross basis of designation to an extraordinary one which will comprise the body, speech and mind of the Buddha that the practitioner will become at the end of the Completion Stage.

It should be clear that this 'shift' can only occur if one has carefully cultivated the correct view of Emptiness as is taught in the Madhyamika system of Arya Nagarjuna. Thus, in intense meditation while in solitary retreat, one concentrates on impending death, the intermediate state, and the rebirth that will follow as the path to the Three Bodies of the Buddha that one will become. Death into the Dharmakaya, the intermediate state into the Sambhogakaya, and rebirth into the Nirmanakaya.

TANTRIC SYMBOLISM: A TYPICAL TANTRIC DEITY

Deities of Highest Secret Mantra are usually of three types—peaceful, wrathful and very wrathful. All are manifestly or symbolically in union with their respective consorts. The guru, on gauging the disciple's emotional and intellectual make-up, will usually choose a suitable deity (or deities) and, during the initiation, will introduce the disciple to the deity and vice versa. The guru will also point out a suitable external environment to meditate on the chosen deity. Forbidding places like isolated cremation grounds and wild, fearsome forests are recommended for meditating on fierce deities that emphasize the energy of wrath. On the other hand, beautiful gardens and orchards, ornamented with lakes and pools, are recommended for meditating on deities who emphasize the energy of lust.

A typical Tantric deity of Highest Secret Mantra would have the colour of one of the five Buddha families to which it belongs. It could be deep space-blue—the colour of Buddha Akshobhya, the purified aggregate of consciousness. This deity would have a stern or wrathful expression, displaying four sharp fangs, symbolizing that it has overcome the four demons.[1] He would have the 'third eye' in the centre of the forehead, denoting his ultimate non-dual vision as distinct from the dualism symbolized by two normal eyes. His long hair, some of which would be falling in curling tresses on his shoulders, would be tied up in a top-knot characteristic of Buddhas, symbolizing his status as 'lord of Yogis'. He would be wearing a diadem of five desiccated skulls, signifying that although he has killed the five principal delusions, he uses them in order to subdue and tame evil sentient beings.

The deity's body is ornamented with six types of 'mudras' or bone-ornaments such as armbands, bracelets, anklets, waistband with tassles, earrings and a warrior's 'belt' that crosses on the front and back of the chest—showing his attainment of the six perfections of the Paramitayana. His two or more arms would hold symbolic implements like the male Vajra, symbolizing 'skilfull means' (Sanskrit: *Upayakaushalya*), and the female bell, symbolizing the wisdom of Emptiness. He would be wearing a garland of 108 freshly-severed heads, indicating his transcendence over the 108 categories of pure and impure phenomena. He would be wearing a tiger skin loin-cloth to symbolize his destruction of the tiger of anger. He would be in the 'warrior's posture', with the left leg bent and the right leg outstretched (or vice versa) to show which of the two major side-channels, the right or left, is emphasized in practice. He would be trampling upon specific worldly gods to indicate the particular internal and external 'demons' that are overcome by meditating on that specific Buddha-deity.

The male-deity is in union with a female consort who clings to him with one or both arms wrapped around his neck, and one or both legs wrapped around his torso. She is similar in demeanour to the male, and wears the same kinds of ornaments and wields similar implements. She is not a separate deity from the male—both male and female deities are the simultaneous forms assumed by the same formless, enlightened awareness, which expresses its blissful status by manifesting as a perfect male in perfect union with a perfect female. Their sexual union also denotes that lust is to be taken as a path.

Both deities stand on the red and white discs of the sun and moon, in the corolla of a gigantic lotus, signifying that mastery over the red and white drops, and the chakras in which they abide, has been attained.

The central father-mother deity couple may be surrounded by varying numbers of deity couples, forming their retinue, each of which symbolizes the enlightened attributes of the central deity-couple. For example, the central deity-couple could denote the Fundamental Mind of Clear Light (symbolized by the male), and its associated wind-energy (symbolized by the female). They could be surrounded by four yoginis who signify the four primary wind-energies of the elements that arise from the root-wind-at the centre. The entire arrangement could indicate the heart-chakra of the meditator. The central deity-couple and retinue (called the resident mandala) would abide in a vast 'celestial-mansion' (called the residence mandala), which, in general, consists of a square, five-layered walled building, with four ornate gateways, in the four cardinal directions.

These 'residence mandalas' are described in great detail in Tantric texts, right down to the number, shape and colour of the awnings, balustrades and arches, all of which denote the detailed facets of the Enlightened mind and form. These mandalas range from simple four-walled, four-gate structures with one to five deities inside, to complex 'clusters' of mandalas within mandalas, with many deities, such as the intricate Kalachakra mandala with 722 deities.

The residence mandala rests on an 'immovable' six-point Vajra, whose four points extend in the four cardinal directions and the axis extends down to the 'golden foundations' of the square 'earth-mandala', which, in turn, rests on a circular 'water mandala', which rests on a triangular 'fire mandala', which is placed on a semi-circular 'wind-mandala'.[2] The whole is contained in the pure space of subtle consciousness. Through meditation on such a pure, empty mandala, the Deity Yoga of the Generation Stage of Highest Secret Mantra breaks the meditator's fixation on the apparent absolute existence of an 'ordinary' subject, in an 'ordinary' objective world.

DEITY YOGA

> *Rupam shunyata*
> *Shunyataiva rupam*
> *(Form is emptiness, emptiness is form.)*
>
> —Heart Sutra

The principal aim of the Tantric meditator while engaging in practices of Highest Secret Mantra is to attain and manifest the omnipresent and immortal Rupakaya in order to teach and guide sentient beings on the path of virtue, liberation and enlightenment. This is possible because the Rupakaya is beyond dualistic space-time and can appear at will, effortlessly, in the ordinary space-time worlds of ignorant sentient beings, in accordance with their needs and karma.

In the Tantric texts, this is explained by comparing the Buddha's omniscient, formless Enlightened mind (the Dharmakaya) to the open sky; the Buddha's actual immortal body of 'Perfect Rapture' (Sambhogakaya) to the radiant full moon; and the individual bodies of teachers and gurus that appear in the worlds of sentient beings as the many reflections of that full moon in bodies of water on earth. Thus, the Tantric meditator, motivated by great compassion, seeks the distinctive Tantric methods (which are not taught in the Sutras), to attain this Rupakaya for benefiting all sentient beings. Deity Yoga is the basis for attaining such a transcendent form.

In the Generation Stage, the meditator prepares to assume the transcendent form of the deity through visualization, and in the Completion Stage, this visualized perfect form and mind is actually attained through the yogas of the channels, winds and drops. Deity Yoga forms part of the Tantric warrior's initial preparation to combat and defeat the demon of uncontrolled death. Thus, one who practises these yogas equips oneself to prepare and deal with one's impending death. To the extent to which one can gain proficiency in these (and subsequent) yogas before death comes, to that extent, one will be able not only to face death with equanimity but will also be able to actually control and use the process of death to fulfil one's vow to manifest the Rupakaya for the benefit of all sentient beings. Deity Yoga sets the stage for dealing directly, and at the deepest level, with those two aspects of our existence which society considers hidden, secret and taboo—our sexuality and our death.

Deity Yoga comprises the meditative cultivation of two factors—Divine Appearance and Divine Identity. The cultivation of Divine Appearance in intense meditation is like conscious controlled dreaming while still awake, where one trains to operate on the subtle mental plane, consciously projecting a divine appearance of oneself as a divine male-female couple, retinue and residence. Since the appearance of the divine reality is a conscious mental projection, one is at all times aware of its emptiness. In other words, the meditator trains to cognize the two truths of emptiness and form, simultaneously, with one consciousness. Since the appearing forms are male-female deities in sexual union, this simultaneous cognition of the two truths is combined with bliss in a facsimile of the ultimate enlightened state of mind. With this divine blissful appearance as the basis of designation, the meditator designates a divine identity thinking, 'This is me', 'I am of the nature of this adamantine body, speech and mind'. In this way, the meditator rapidly accumulates the two 'accumulations' of merit (*punya*) and wisdom (*pragya*), which would take 'three countless aeons' of time in the non-Tantric vehicle of the Sutras.

The vision of oneself as the deity is built up step by step, with effort over months or years of daily meditation in four sessions. Initially, one has to be satisfied with only a hazy (often dark) image of the deity-couple. One works slowly, making each part, ornament and detail clear and vivid, starting first with one deity of the divine couple, then turning one's attention to the other deity, and then the retinue and the residence mandala. Eventually, the meditator builds up a vivid, three-dimensional vision of the complete divine mandala as the basis of designation of a divine 'I'.

When the meditator reaches the stage where one can instantly perceive the entire mandala without having to build it up bit by bit, then one has reached an advanced level of mental purification and success. Although the ordinary world and one's ordinary aggregates, which are the result of past karma, continue to appear to the waking mind, the meditator no longer strongly identifies with that ordinary appearance as the basis of designation of 'I'. Internally, one constantly perceives the divine mandala as one's identification with it grows.

Initially, the mundane world with its absolute appearance is real, while one's divine vision is an unreal mental fabrication. However, as the vision becomes more vivid and clear, the meditator's attention shifts from the gross plane to the subtle level of consciousness where depth transformation is possible in a manner impossible during the gross, waking period of the 'ordinary' world. The meditator cultivates the divine vision in formal seated meditation sessions. In the post-meditation period, one maintains one's 'divine appearance' and 'divine identity' and enjoys the various objects of the senses as sensory offerings to the Deity. Thus, even daily activities like eating and walking become rituals for the accumulation of merit and wisdom.

STOPPING BLISS

Buddha has taught the path of celibacy as the basic foundation of the spiritual path to Enlightenment. Taking formal vows of sexual abstinence (Sanskrit: *Brahmacharya*), the life of a renunciant Bhikshu or Bhikshuni is considered ideal for devoting all one's time and energy to the spiritual path. Celibacy here would mean giving up all sexual activity whatsoever, including any kind of self-stimulation, so that one does not deliberately cause the emission of regenerative fluid[3] during orgasm. Buddha has recommended such celibacy not because he considered sexual activity to be wrong or sinful but because the basic aim of all Buddhists is to attain liberation (Nirvana) from compulsive cyclic existence.

One of the principal causes keeping us bound in cyclic existence is desire-attachment to gross sensory pleasures. And of all such pleasures, sexual pleasure is the strongest where all five senses are intently engaged. Since we cannot live without food, shelter and clothing, Buddha has allowed renunciant monks and nuns to use these in simple moderation. But since we can live without sexual activity, Buddha has recommended complete sexual abstinence for renunciant monks and nuns, while allowing lay practitioners and householders to engage in normal sexual activity, free from sexual misconduct.

Sexual misconduct is generally defined as the 'Four Wrongs'—wrong object, i.e. an unsuitable object of attention, like someone else's spouse, an unwilling person, a celibate monk or nun, a person of the same sex; wrong organ, i.e. anal and oral sex are considered sexual misconduct; wrong place, i.e. a public place likely to offend others, or a sacred place such as temples and monasteries; wrong time, when one's partner is ill or pregnant or has taken temporary vows of celibacy.

However, since both celibate and non-celibate yogis and yoginis can practise the path of Highest Secret Mantra, a distinction has to be made concerning their modes of practice. The austere celibate practice of Tantra is considered safer although it takes longer. It is compared to a gradual, safe ascent up a mountain pass that avoids dangers like vertical cliffs, ravines and rock faces. The non-celibate practice of 'overwhelming means' is compared to a dangerous vertical ascent that does not avoid dangers like cliffs and therefore requires greater skill and strength.

The completely celibate practice of Highest Secret Mantra, as exemplified by the life of Lama Tsongkhapa, does not lead to Complete Enlightenment while alive, for one must wait for the Clear Light of Death in order to manifest the Dharmakaya and Rupakaya. On the other hand, the non-celibate practice of Highest Secret Mantra, as exemplified by the lives of many of the Eighty-Four Mahasiddhas of India, is the only path that can lead to complete manifestation of the Dharmakaya and Rupakaya while one is alive. In Tibetan Buddhism, a compromise is often resorted to where celibate yogis and yoginis who have reached the advanced 'mind-isolation' level of the Completion Stages (to be explained in the subsequent section on the Completion Stage), are allowed to practise with an actual consort. At that advanced level of wind-energy control, there is no possibility of emitting the regenerative fluid uncontrollably as one can sustain intense levels of bliss with complete control.

However, whether one is a celibate or a non-celibate practitioner of Highest Secret Mantra, when one starts meditating, in vivid detail, on oneself as a divine couple in sexual union during Deity Yoga, sexual energy is bound to be aroused. One must learn control in order to sustain higher and higher levels of bliss without emission or orgasm, since that would immediately terminate the entire blissful experience.

Sustaining higher and higher levels of sexual bliss is the heart of Highest Secret Mantra because the more blissful a mind is, the more focused, subtle and aloof it is, and it can become a powerful means of meditating on emptiness. It is said that one moment of such meditation, that is a union of bliss and emptiness, is equivalent to many thousand sessions of meditation on emptiness without such bliss. Further, when such a mind of bliss-emptiness is used as the basis of divine appearance, the resultant union of Bliss+Emptiness+Form is the actual cultivation of the Deity Yoga of the Generation Stage of Highest Secret Mantra.

Thus, a secret mantra meditator who uses the path of bliss must have the prerequisite abilities to, first, turn the mind immediately to an authentic image of emptiness without any further reasoning, analysis or cogitation. Secondly, one must be able to unite such a wisdom-consciousness with the sustained bliss of sexual arousal. Thirdly, one should be able to generate such a mind of bliss-emptiness into the vivid appearance of a divine resident and residence mandala.

In order to possess such abilities, the meditator should have spent time and effort to, first, generate an authentic image of the profound emptiness through the path of Madhyamika reasoning and analysis, such that one has reached the level of 'inferential cognition' of emptiness, which is irreversible. Secondly, one should have learned to sustain sexual bliss without emission through force of will power. And if one practises with an actual partner, then through such means as cooperation from a skilful partner, positional variation, and diet. Thirdly, one should have generated a vivid image of oneself as the divine couple through solitary, seated meditative visualization. Sustaining sexual bliss without emission is crucial and very difficult as all beings are bound in cyclic existence because of their deep attachment to the bliss of emission at orgasm.

The Tantric meditator is expected to renounce this attachment even while engaging in intense sexual activity (imagined or actual). Since the meditator has not yet attained control over the 'downward-voiding wind' (one of the five root-winds, which is responsible for emission at orgasm, and control over which is attained only in the Completion Stage), one has to be careful not to break the Tantric commitment to refrain from emission even in one's dreams.

It should be evident that the kind of sexual activity being referred to in Highest Secret Mantra is very different from the ordinary sexual intercourse of ignorant beings. In fact, it would be quite correct to say that in Highest Secret Mantra, one learns to put one's sexual faculty to its highest possible use.

STOPPING DEATH

> '*Homage to Amitabha, Buddha of*
> *limitless light—the Dharmakaya.*'
>
> —The Bardo Thodrol

In the Deity Yoga of the Generation Stage of Highest Secret Mantra, one not only meditates on the form of the Deity as the basis of designation of a divine identity, but also on the mind (Dharmakaya) and speech-energy (Sambhogakaya) of the Deity as a composite basis of designation of oneself as the Deity. To generate the Dharmakaya-mind of the Deity, one dissolves one's ordinary mind in a process that mimics the actual dissolution of the individual gross mind that occurs naturally at death. The meditator, in seated meditation, visualizes a tiny blue HUNG-syllable (ý·) at one's heart-point.

This HUNG-syllable emits a flash of brilliant blue light that dissolves one's ordinary world into blue light. The sphere of light then implodes inwards and absorbs into one's body; the body dissolves into blue light and absorbs inwards into the HUNG-syllable at the heart-point. Simultaneously, one visualizes the internal sign of the dissolution of the earth-element wind-energy—a shimmering mirage-like vision. With one's mind focused on the HUNG-syllable, one imagines the U-symbol (ᵂ) of the HUNG dissolving into the H-symbol (ɳ). Simultaneously, one visualizes the internal sign of the dissolution of the water-element wind-energy—a vision of dense billowing smoke, filling space. Next, the H-symbol (ɳ) dissolves into the horizontal line. Simultaneously, one visualizes the internal sign of the dissolution of the fire-element wind-energy—a vision of swirling sparks, like fireflies. Next, the horizontal line dissolves into the crescent (.) and, simultaneously, one visualizes the internal sign for the dissolution of the air-element wind-energy—a vision like the light of a sputtering candle about to go out.

All the gross levels of mind have now subsided and ceased. The meditator then visualizes the emergence of the three subtle levels of mind. As the crescent of the HUNG dissolves into the drop (¿) above, one visualizes the emergence of the subtle 'mind of white-appearance'—like space filled with white light. As the drop dissolves into the 'Nada' (squiggle) at the top of the drop, there emerges the subtler 'mind of red-increase' like space filled with red light. Then, as the Nada dissolves, there emerges the subtler 'mind of black near-attainment'—like space filled with black darkness.

When the squiggle has completely dissolved, there emerges the very subtle 'Mind of Clear Light'—like limitless and centre-less space filled with clear, colourless light. With this very subtle, all-pervasive Clear-Light Mind, the meditator focuses on the emptiness of this very mind, thereby 'sealing' it with the seal of emptiness. Then thinking, 'I am the omniscient Dharmakaya of the Deity,' the practitioner generates the divine pride of having actualized the omniscient Dharmakaya. This meditation is called 'Taking Death as the Path to the Dharmakaya.' What is visualized here is attained in the Completion Stage, where the omniscient Dharmakaya of all the Buddhas is attained, and compulsive, uncontrolled death is forever terminated.

STOPPING THE INTERMEDIATE STATE

> '*Homage to the peaceful and wrathful*
> *Lotus–Deities—the Sambhogakaya.*'
> —The Bardo Thodrol

Having generated a space-like vision of the Clear-Light Mind focused on Emptiness, the meditator maintains the divine pride of the Dharmakaya. Then remembering one's Bodhichitta motivation to manifest the Rupakaya for the benefit of others, the meditator spontaneously rises from this space-like vision into a shaft of light, or a seed-syllable such as HUNG (ý·). Thinking, 'I am the Sambhogakaya of the Deity,' the practitioner generates the divine pride of having attained the immortal Sambhogakaya. This meditation is called 'Taking the intermediate state as the path to the Sambhogakaya.'

In the Completion Stage, when the meditator actualizes the 'Ultimate-Meaning Clear Light' (Sanskrit: *Paramarthabhaswara*), the next moment, one will arise in the immortal 'Body of Perfect Rapture' (Sambhogakaya), complete with retinue and residence mandalas. One will then forever terminate the uncontrolled dream-like visions of the intermediate state between death in one life, and rebirth in another.

STOPPING UNCONTROLLED REBIRTH

'Homage to Padmasambhava, protector of all beings—
the Nirmanakaya.'

—The Bardo Thodrol

Maintaining the pride of being the Sambhogakaya of the Deity, the meditator reminds oneself of one's Bodhichitta motivation to benefit all beings. Seeing how the Sambhogakaya is perceivable only by advanced Tantric yogins and Eighth to Tenth-ground Bodhisattvas, one resolves to arise in the Nirmanakaya of the deity to benefit all beings, everywhere, in all realms of cyclic existence. Mimicking the process of rebirth, one imagines oneself as the seed-syllable HUNG, descending on a lotus-seat with moon and sun discs, symbolizing the sperm and ovum of one's future parents, in the womb of one's future mother. Then in the manner of 'a fish leaping out of water,' one arises as the male-female deity, with retinue and residence mandalas. This is the main meditation of Deity Yoga where the meditator focuses intently to make the divine appearance of oneself as the divine mandala vivid and clear in all detail. When the mind tires of visualization, one rests while reciting the mantra of the Deity.

In the profound yoga of the post-meditation period, the meditator maintains the divine-appearance and divine pride, creatively imagining all male things in the world to be emanations of the male deity, and all female things in the world to be emanations of the female deity. This meditation is called 'taking rebirth as the path to the Nirmanakaya'. In the Completion Stage, when the meditator actualizes the Final Union of the Two Truths, one will attain the ability to take deliberate rebirth in male and female bodies simultaneously in many worlds, in order to guide and benefit sentient beings throughout space and time.

This description of the Generation Stage practice of Highest Secret Mantra is a general one, with many variations in individual Tantras. Before embarking on the practice of Deity Yoga of a particular deity, one should be intimately familiar with details of the sadhanas of those deities. Lama Tsongkhapa has criticized some of the Tantric schools for not paying sufficient attention to the practice of the Generation Stage, emphasizing that the mind of the practitioner must be first matured and purified by visualizations of the Generation Stage before embarking on the very advanced yogas of the Completion Stage. Otherwise, not only is there the great danger of committing an error but also the peril of the practitioner being afflicted with wind-energy disorders which can lead to serious physical diseases.

Having received the teachings and empowerments from one's Guru, initially, one pays greater emphasis on the Generation Stage, spending very little time on the Completion Stage practices. Then as one's mind becomes more focused and pliable, one decreases one's effort on the Generation Stage, while simultaneously increasing one's effort at the Completion Stage. Eventually, one's entire energy and focus shifts to the Completion Stage. When one can instantly evoke the vision of the Deity in complete and vivid detail, one has reached the accomplishment of the 'coarse' level of the Generation Stage. When one can reduce the entire mandala of the deity to the size of a pea without losing any clarity or detail or expand it to fill all of space, then one has reached the accomplishment of the 'subtle' level of the Generation Stage Yoga. By then, one's mind would be purified of its fixation on and identification with the gross mundane world, and with such a purified and pliable mind, one would be ready to take on the very profound yogas of the Completion Stage.

SAMPANNA KRAM — THE COMPLETION STAGE

'*From the Celestial space of Samantabhadri,*
The uncreated mandala, Samantabhadra, arises.
In its arising, there is nothing that arises.
The Supreme Bliss of father, mother and offspring
Is spontaneously perfect.'

—Nagarjuna

'The Dharmadhatu, which is free from all (conceptual) elaboration, is also called "Tathagatagarbha". All schools of Vajrayana, both the older and the more recent, speak about this Buddha Nature, the Wisdom of Clear Light. Because it cannot be established to have true existence or to be independent (of the perceiver), it is termed "free from elaboration". In essence it is primordially pure, by nature it is spontaneously present. It is this Buddha Nature that serves as the ground for all Samsara and Nirvana, a vast expanse, within which all elaborations—the phenomena of Samsara and Nirvana—arise and subside. Pure by its very nature . . . an expanse that permeates everything and within which everything is contained and Complete.'

—His Holiness the Dalai Lama

The Completion Stage of Highest Secret Mantra (also called the 'Perfection Stage') is the summation of the sequential path (Tibetan: *Lam-Rim*) that leads to the Complete Enlightenment of a Buddha, adorned with the Three Bodies (Kayas). All prior steps—from taking Refuge in the Three

Jewels, to generating renunciation, generating the Highest Aspiration of Bodhichitta, the inferential cognition of the Profound Emptiness, the three lower Tantras and the Generation Stage of Highest Secret Mantra—are preliminaries that prepare the yogi to practise the Completion Stage which leads to the realization of the Three Kayas of Enlightenment.

Different schools of Tibetan Buddhism break up the practice of the Completion Stage differently, with there being three major traditions—those of the Older Translation Schools (Nyingma-pa), who divide the practice into three phases of Maha, Anu and Atiyogas; the New Translation Schools who follow the basic system of the Guhyasamaja Tantra which separates the practice into six (or five) phases; and the unique Kalachakra System which breaks up the practice into six phases distinct from the Guhyasamaja. This discussion of the Completion Stage is based on a popular system followed by the Kagyu and Geluk schools, the 'Six Yogas of Naropa', which amalgamates practices from the Mother Tantras of Hevajra and Heruka into the basic pattern of the Guhyasamaja.

The six phases of the Completion Stage are: (1) isolating the essence of form (or body isolation), (2) isolating the essence of energy (or speech isolation), (3) isolating the essence of mind (or mind isolation), (4) the actual Clear Light—the Ultimate Truth, (5) the actual Apparitional Body—the Conventional Truth, (6) Yuganaddha—the Final Union of the Two Truths.

ISOLATING THE ESSENCE OF FORM

In this phase, one unites the practice of the Generation Stage with that of the Completion Stage. During the Deity Yoga of the Generation Stage, the meditator has isolated one's sense of self ('I') from ordinary appearance by generating oneself vividly and clearly as the perfect form of the deity, consort, retinue and residence mandalas, thereby blocking the mind's fixation on oneself as a gross ordinary being in an ordinary world. However, for the Deity to be 'Complete', the vision of the deity must not only be a union of emptiness and form but must also be a union of bliss-emptiness and form. Thus, the deity must be a form-manifestation of a blissful consciousness that is focused on emptiness. Here, 'bliss' refers to the unique 'Great Bliss' (Sanskrit: *Mahasukkha*) that arises exclusively in the Completion Stage when the winds are consciously brought to enter, abide and cease in the Central Channel.

Until now, the Generation Stage meditator has used only a facsimile of this 'Great Bliss' through visualizing oneself as a male and female deity in sexual union. The bliss arising from such a vision is used as a substitute for the 'Great Bliss' of the Completion Stage. To experience this actual 'Great Bliss', one must utilize a Completion Stage technique such as 'Chandali Yoga'. This can cause the winds to enter, abide and cease in the Central Channel, thereby melting the white drop in the head-chakra and causing it to flow down in a completely controlled manner within the central channel, giving rise to 'Great Bliss', which is said to be many times more intense than the bliss of the most intense sexual orgasm. When such a sustained, intensely blissful consciousness is focused on emptiness, the resultant consciousness is called the 'Mahamudra' (Great Seal) that is the 'Union of Bliss and Emptiness.' When such a consciousness altruistically manifests as the vision of the perfect form of a male and female deity in sexual union, that is the actual 'isolation of the essence of Form' of the Completion Stage.

CHANDALI YOGA

'*Om Namah Vajravarahi, Mahayogini, Kameshwari Khage Hum Hum phat.*'
(*Om Homage to Vajravarahi, the great Yogini, who overpowers the goddess of lust Hum Hum phat.*)
—Eight Verses of Praise to Vajravarahi

The word 'Chandali' (Tibetan: *Tummo*) means 'Fierce Woman' and refers to practices associated with the 'female pole' in the dual male-female polarity of one's own body. According to the Tantras, this 'female pole' is located at the red drop, which is present in the centre of the sixty-four petal navel-chakra, situated at a width of about four fingers behind the navel. This red drop, derived from a portion of the original red-drop (ovum) of one's mother at the time of one's conception in this life, is responsible for body heat, digestion, the increase of the red drops in the body, for the 'heat' of sexual arousal and sexual orgasm.

In the Tantric iconography of Deity Yoga, this drop (and its heat) is personified as the female deity, Vajra Yogini (Indestructible Yogini) or Vajra Varahi (Indestructible Sow). She is usually depicted as a blood-red, naked woman, adorned with six tantric mudras (bone ornaments), holding a kapala (skull-cup) full of blood in the left hand, symbolizing the wisdom of bliss and emptiness, and a katri (cleaver knife) in her right hand, denoting the termination of conceptual elaboration. She is also depicted as the divine consort of Sri Heruka Chakrasamvara, lord of the Heruka Mandala. As a whole, she symbolizes the primordial wisdom of bliss and emptiness—the very heart of the Tantric path.

The union of the meditator's mind with the Great Bliss personified by this deity is brought about by gaining control over the functioning of the red drop located at one's navel-chakra. Chandali Yoga, which has many benefits, is the foundation of the rest of the Completion Stage. For those who have not yet completely attained an 'abiding calm' (Shamatha) of the gross mind through the techniques of Sutra or the Generation Stage, Chandali Yoga confers this quality very quickly so that all sensory distractions to the 'outside' are pacified. One can then hold one's mind single-pointedly to a subtle internal object for indefinite periods of time.

Most importantly, this practice confers upon the meditator complete control over the 'downward-voiding' wind-energy (one of the five root wind-energies) which is responsible for uncontrolled emission during sexual orgasm. Through gaining control over this wind-energy, the meditator can now sustain deep states of bliss without any fear of uncontrolled emission. It is said that the successful practise of this yoga improves one's health and vitality and slows down the ageing process. It is the principal pathway for attaining the supernormal powers (Sanskrit: *Siddhis*) of the Tantric path. The practice of 'Chandali Yoga' was taught by the Buddha in the Hevajra Root Tantra.

In order to practise this yoga, one has to be initiated into one of the principal Mother Tantras, such as Heruka Chakrasamvara or Hevajra. One then has to receive explicit verbal instructions from one's guru on the visualizations of this yoga, along with an actual demonstration of the six (or more) physical Hatha-Yoga exercises, which are to be done in conjunction with intense meditative focusing.

As with the rest of the entire path, Chandali Yoga is practised in a definite sequence of steps. First, in the meditation session, one generates oneself as the deity of the Generation Stage, but alone without consort or retinue, with only one face, two arms and two legs (unlike in the Generation Stage, where most Highest Secret Mantra deities have many heads, arms and legs). Then, instead of focusing on the external features of oneself as the deity, one focuses on the internal features of the deity's energy-system of Channels and Chakras.

To do this, one visualizes one's deity-body as being completely hollow, like the inside of an inflated body shaped balloon. Having stabilized this vision of a hollow body, the meditator next visualizes the Central Channel, the 'avadhuti', extending from the point of mid-brow to a width of four fingers below the navel-chakra. When this channel has been clearly 'established' so that one can actually 'see' it with one's mind's eye, both inside and outside, one then turns one's attention to the two red and white side-channels, the 'lalana' and 'rasana'. These lie parallel to the central channel, to its right and left respectively, and coil around it, forming one knot each at the crown, throat and navel chakras, and three knots each at the heart-chakra.

Having established this channel system, the meditator actually enters the central channel in the form of a tiny, luminous drop of light that moves up and down the central channel, seeing it and the chakras from the inside, like travelling up and down in an elevator. Next, one establishes the four principal drops located in the centre of each of the four chakras. These drops are visualized as tiny (the size of a mustard seed), luminous Sanskrit (or Tibetan) seed-syllables such as white OM at the crown-chakra, red AH at the throat-chakra, blue HUM at the heart-chakra, and red short – A (Tibetan: *A-Thung*) at the navel-chakra.

It is vital that each of these drops be clearly established so that one can actually merge one's mind with the seed-syllable, as if one is the seed-syllable standing in the centre of the spokes of the chakra. This kind of intense meditative focus is necessary in order to gain control over the four states of waking (white drop in the head-chakra), dreaming (red drop in the throat-chakra), deep sleep (red-white drop at the heart-chakra), and sexual orgasm (red drop at the navel-chakra).

When these four drops have been clearly established, the practitioner turns one's intensely focused, laser-like mind, to the red-drop at the navel-chakra. Immersing one's mind into this red drop, the meditator consciously switches it on, igniting the 'inner fire' of Chandali, the fierce woman. This 'inner fire' is visualized as a needle-point of blue incandescence, which the meditator consciously directs up the central channel, keeping the heat strictly within the central channel and directing it up to the white drop located in the crown-chakra, which forms the male polarity of the body. This causes the white drop to 'melt' and flow down within the central channel, giving rise to the 'Great Bliss' of the Completion Stage.

During ordinary sexual intercourse, a process similar to the above process occurs. Due to the union and movement of the sexual organs, the red drop at the navel is ignited, giving off the 'heat' of sexual arousal. This heat moves up the side channels, causing the white drop to melt and flow down the side channels but not in the central channel. This flowing down of the white drop gives rise to the bliss of ordinary sexual intercourse. Due to its moving down the side channels, this flow cannot be consciously controlled and, eventually, the white drops reach the sexual organ where they are emitted uncontrollably.

However, during the 'inner fire' meditation of Chandali Yoga, the heat is strictly confined within the central channel, causing the white drop to flow within the central channel where complete control over its movement can be attained. Furthermore, this flow within the central channel gives rise to a deep, focused and intense bliss, quite different from the bliss of ordinary sexual intercourse, which is superficial and very weak in comparison. It is this intense, sustained, highly focused mind of Great Bliss that is then concentrated on emptiness.

Thus, the 'inner fire' meditation of Chandali Yoga unites the subtle mind of the meditator with Great Bliss. It gathers the wind-energies, causing them to enter, abide and cease within the Central Channel at the navel-chakra, thereby giving rise to a semblance of the eight internal signs that occur at death. This Great Bliss is increased in intensity with the yoga of the 'Four Blisses', and the eight signs of the dissolution of the winds are blended with the 'Three Bodies' during waking, dreaming and deep sleep in the yoga of the 'Nine Blendings'.

THE FOUR BLISSES

During this yoga, which can only be practised after one has ignited the 'inner fire' of the Fierce Woman, the meditator learns to sustain and bear higher and higher levels of bliss focused on emptiness, in a phased manner, in preparation for experiencing the primordial bliss of the Completely Enlightened Mind. As the white drop in the head-chakra melts and flows down within the central channel, its flow is consciously arrested and halted at each of the chakras, thereby giving rise to the Four Blisses, where each level of bliss is deeper and more intense than the previous level.

Thus, when the white drop in the head-chakra melts and flows down to the throat-chakra, its flow is arrested there and one experiences the level of Great Bliss. Having conjoined this mind of 'Bliss' with emptiness, one allows the drop to flow from the throat-chakra to the heart-chakra and arrests its flow there and one experiences the second level of Bliss called 'Supreme Bliss'. Keeping one's mind focused on emptiness, one allows the white drop to descend to the navel-chakra. Arresting its flow there, one experiences 'special Bliss'. Then allowing the drop to flow from the navel-chakra to the tip of the sexual organ, one experiences 'innate bliss' (Sanskrit: *Sahaja-ananda*).

Since by now the meditator would have attained control over the 'downward voiding' wind-energy, one can not only hold the white drops at the tip of the sexual organ for as long as one likes, but can also actually reverse the flow of the drop back up the Central Channel. Due to this, one experiences the Four Blisses of the ascending drop which are even more intense than the Four Blisses of the descending drop. It is said that the meditator who can arrest and reverse the flow of the white drop within the Central Channel attains the supernormal mind-power to arrest and reverse the flow of a river—a feat reportedly performed by many of the Mahasiddhas.

When the white drop is brought up the Central Channel and the 'innate bliss' is conjoined with emptiness, the knots at the chakras are slightly loosened. Due to this, the wind-energies flowing in the two side channels partially enter into the Central Channel, specially at the navel-chakra, where they abide and cease, giving rise to the eight signs from mirage to Clear Light.

THE NINE BLENDINGS

The 'inner fire' of Chandali Yoga is called the foundation of the Completion Stage because when the meditator can penetrate the Central Channel in the manner outlined above, with the Bodhichitta motivation of manifesting the Rupakaya, then one has the key to unlock the sealed doors that lead to the Ultimate Clear Light—the ultimate nature of reality. Now that one can consciously cause the winds to enter, abide, and cease in the Central Channel (although only partially as yet), the meditator can experience what was only visualized during the Generation Stage. This experience is now 'blended' with the yogas of the waking state, the sleeping state and the death-state. To the extent to which one can master this crucial practice, to that extent one will be able to master the process of death, whenever it may come.

THE THREE BLENDINGS DURING WAKING

Now that the meditator can consciously bring the wind-energies to enter, abide, and cease within the Central Channel at the navel-chakra, one can, for the first time, consciously experience in the waking state subtle levels of mind. Thus, in formal meditation sessions, the meditator ignites the 'inner fire' of Chandali, and as one ascends the levels of bliss, the grosser levels of mind absorb into the subtler levels and the eight signs of dissolution of the wind-energies arise. First comes the mirage-like vision as the earth-energy ceases, then the smoke-like vision as the water-energy ceases, then the sparks-like vision as the fire-energy ceases, then the sputtering-lamp-like vision as the air-energy ceases.

The gross levels of dualistic mind cease and the three expansive visions of the subtle levels of mind arise—first the vision of space pervaded by white light, then the vision of space pervaded by red light, then black-darkness. Finally, as the subtle minds absorb and cease, the very subtle Clear-Light Mind becomes manifest. The meditator is mindful of emptiness throughout the process, and as the Clear-Light Mind arises, one meditates on emptiness with this very subtle level of mind, and assumes the 'divine pride' of being the omniscient Dharmakaya. This is called 'Blending With The Dharmakaya' during waking.

Next, remembering one's Bodhichitta motivation to manifest the Rupakaya for the benefit of others, one spontaneously arises as the male-female form of one's personal meditation deity (Yidam). One imagines this form to be snow-white in colour, like the colour of Vajrasattva, the Primordial Heroic Being, which is the actual colour of the Sambhogakaya. Seeing oneself as this male-female form in union, one assumes the divine pride of being the Sambhogakaya of the deity. This is called 'Blending With the Sambhogakaya' during waking.

Then, prior to leaving the meditation session, one resolves to appear in a form that is perceivable by ordinary beings. In a process similar to the re-absorption of the dream-body when we wake from a dream, the meditator reduces the snow-white Sambhogakaya to thumb-size (or smaller) and enters into one's physical form from the fontanelle aperture at the top of the head. Descending the central channel, one abides in the heart-chakra, and assumes the divine pride of being the Nirmanakaya of the Deity. One's

physical form has been visualized as being the coloured form
of the Deity throughout the Generation and Completion
Stages. Thus, while generating the divine pride of being the
Nirmanakaya, one 'Blends With the Nirmanakaya' during
waking.

The Clear-Light Mind, generated through the 'inner fire'
meditation, is not the actual Clear-Light Mind which arises
only during the fourth of the six phases of the Completion
Stage. Since the wind-energies have absorbed only partially
at the navel-chakra, the Clear Light experienced here is
relatively gross and dualistic in comparison to the actual
Clear-Light Mind. The Clear-Light Mind generated through
meditation is called 'the Child Clear Light' which
progressively deepens during each successive phase of the
Completion Stage until in the fourth phase it 're-unites' with
the actual 'Mother Clear Light'.

THE THREE BLENDINGS DURING SLEEP

Within the twenty-four hour cycle, the process of falling
asleep, dreaming and waking up is similar to the process of
dying, arising as the intermediate state being, and taking
rebirth. The former process is reversible because it is partial,
while the latter is irreversible because it is total.

When we fall asleep, the gross wind-energies and their
associated sensory consciousnesses absorb partially into the
heart-chakra and cease within the Central Channel. Due to
this, the phenomenal waking world disappears as the eight
signs of dissolution appear.

The untrained sleeper is completely unaware of these
signs since mindfulness is progressively lost as the gross mind
shuts down. Then, as the last subtle mind of black-darkness
ceases, the 'Mother' Clear Light of sleep arises, similar to

the 'Mother' Clear Light of death which is deeper because all the wind-energies and minds absorb and cease. The untrained sleeper experiences this Clear-Light Mind of sleep as the complete unconscious blankness of a deep dreamless sleep. Then, eventually, the wind-energy of this Clear-Light Mind stirs and moves to the throat-chakra, giving rise to the appearance of the dream-body along with its dream-world. Eventually, the gross wind-energies re-emerge and move to the head-chakra, giving rise to the karmically determined experience of the waking-world.

The trained Secret-Mantra meditator who can consciously cause the wind-energies to absorb into the Central Channel during waking through such techniques as Chandali Yoga, and who can remain aware of emptiness during the eight signs of dissolution up to the Clear Light, attains the power to retain mindfulness during the entire process of falling asleep, dreaming and waking, using each state to blend with the Three Bodies. The process occurs at a much deeper and firmer level than during waking, and one who can experience it, has reached a profound level of realization.

During the blending with sleep, as the Secret Mantra meditator falls asleep, one focuses on the red-drop at the navel-chakra, causing the Chandali fire to arise just as one is falling asleep. Shifting one's attention to the heart-chakra where the wind-energies naturally absorb, one experiences the eight signs of dissolution, from mirage-like to Clear Light, with complete mindfulness of the arising of each sign and of its emptiness.

When the Clear-Light Mind of deep sleep arises, the meditator focuses on emptiness and the two, the subjective Clear-Light Mind of the meditator and the objective emptiness of that mind, blend. Assuming the divine pride of being the omniscient Dharmakaya of one's meditation Deity, one rests in that realization. Then when the wind-energies gather at the throat-chakra and the dream state arises, the meditator is able to arise in the dream-form of the Deity instead of in an ordinary dream body.

In this way, one experiences a subtle physical reality similar to the actual 'apparitional body' that is attained in the fifth of the six phases of the Completion Stage. Since the dream is realistic and vivid, one can actually experience the state of subtle blissful embodiment of the Sambhogakaya, and assuming the divine pride of being the Sambhogakaya is all the more realistic and vivid. This is called blending with the Sambhogakaya during sleep. A skilled meditator can multiply his body many times over and visit the subtle 'pure-lands' of different Buddhas and Buddha-deities and make offerings to them and receive their blessings and empowerments. In this way, even in one's dreams, one can gather vast stores of merit and wisdom.

When the wind-energies eventually stir and gather at the head-chakra, giving rise to the waking state, one's Sambhogakaya Dream-body absorbs into the heart-chakra, and one assumes the divine pride of being the Nirmanakaya of the Deity. Waking up, one has the divine pride of being a 'triple-being', where one's physical body is the Nirmanakaya, in its heart-chakra is the Sambhogakaya, and in its head-chakra is the seed-syllable, symbolic of the formless Dharmakaya.

THE THREE BLENDINGS DURING DEATH

The practitioner of Secret Mantra who has reached a high level of Blending with the Three Bodies during sleep has achieved an advanced level of practice. Such a person meditates continuously on the Three Bodies that constitute the Completely Enlightened State; one does this twenty-four hours a day, waking, dreaming and sleeping. If untimely death, ordained by one's past karma, does not strike, and if one can continue practising the remaining phases of the Completion Stage, Complete Enlightenment as the Three Bodies (Trikaya) is certain. One would then bypass the experience of ordinary death, since one would have actualized the Ultimate Clear-Light Mind and transformed it into the immortal Dharmakaya mind of a Completely Enlightened Buddha.

One's physical body, which is the effect of past ignorant karma, could be disposed of in several ways. One could physically 'fly off' to a pure land in the manner of 'sky-farers' (*Dakas* and *Dakinis*) as was done by many yogis such as the Indian Mahasiddha Chimbu-pada (third century A.D.) or Guru Padmasambhava. Or one could dematerialize one's body and disappear in a flash of light, absorbing into the subtle Sambhogakaya form which is not perceivable by ordinary beings, as was done by Nagarjuna's disciple Arya-Deva. Or one could 'discard' the physical body at its natural karmically determined death, as was done by most of the great masters like the venerable Yogi Mila-Repa.

However, for those yogis whose practice is interrupted by untimely death before they have attained the third of the six phases of the Completion Stage, there are two possibilities. The accomplished yogi who has attained deep experience of the blendings during waking and sleeping will be able to transform his 'Mother Clear Light' of death into the Dharmakaya, thereby completely 'bypassing' the experience of the ordinary intermediate state and subsequent rebirth. Such a one would attain Complete Enlightenment as a Buddha during the process of death. The not so-accomplished yogi will, however, experience the three states of death, intermediate state, and rebirth and will have the unique opportunity to practise the Three Blendings during death. Such a yogi would either attain Enlightenment in the intermediate state or, failing which, will be able to take voluntary rebirth in favourable conditions so as to continue where one left off in the previous life.

For such a yogi, when death strikes untimely, and all the wind-energies and their associated consciousnesses are absorbed completely into the heart-chakra and cease there, the eight signs of dissolution arise vividly and completely. Recognizing them by virtue of practising the blending during sleep, one will be able to retain mindfulness of each sign and its emptiness. When the very subtle 'Mother Clear Light' of death arises, the practitioner, by meditating on emptiness with this subtle mind, is able to blend the experience with the Dharmakaya as in the blending during sleep. Then, when the very subtle wind-energy stirs, instead of arising into a karmically determined intermediate-state body, the meditator will arise into a semblance of the male-female form of the meditation Deity.

Consciously choosing an appropriate womb, one will enter into the sperm-ovum mixture of one's future parents. Holding the divine-pride and appearance of oneself as the deity, such a meditator will abide in one's mother's womb until birth as if in the 'Celestial Mansion' of the deity. Even though one appears as an ordinary baby to others at birth, one will have the 'divine appearance' and pride of being the 'triple-being' Deity. In this way, one will be able to retain the continuity of awareness throughout the process of death, intermediate state, and rebirth, without forgetting one's knowledge and practice in the former life. Such meditators are often able to recollect their former lives and are often recognized by their gurus who reinstal them in their former practice. Such yogis are called Tulkus in the Tibetan language.

In order to practise the 'Blendings with Death', it is necessary to be free from negative states of mind such as anger, hatred, fear or attachment while dying. Since death can come suddenly, violently, and in many terrifying forms, it is crucial for the Tantric practitioner to be ever vigilant during every moment of one's life. It is best to die in a meditative frame of mind, such as while practising Chandali Yoga or whatever level of meditative practice one has reached in one's life. At the least, one should try to die in a virtuous frame of mind. And this will depend entirely on how well one has practised the teachings of one's guru while alive.

The yoga of the 'isolation of the essence of form', the first of the six phases of the Completion Stage, is basically accomplished when the meditator can 'seal' the 'divine appearance' of oneself as the Deity with the 'Great Seal' (Mahamudra) of Bliss-emptiness. Such a state can be arrived at by causing the wind-energies to enter, abide and cease within the Central Channel through such practices as Chandali Yoga.

ISOLATING THE ESSENCE OF ENERGY

Once the meditator gains proficiency in causing the wind-energies to enter, abide and cease within the Central Channel through focusing on a secondary chakra like the navel-chakra, the focus shifts to the primary heart-chakra which is the seat of the Fundamental Innate Mind of Clear Light and its associated subtle wind-energy. These are the focus of the rest of the five phases of the Completion Stage, where the Fundamental Innate Mind of Clear Light is transformed into the Dharmakaya Mind, and its associated wind-energy into the Rupakaya Form of a fully Enlightened Buddha.

During the yogas of the 'Isolation of the essence of energy' (also called 'Speech Isolation'), the yogi initially brings about the loosening of the six-fold knot at the heart-chakra, and 'isolates' the very subtle wind-energy of the Clear-Light Mind from its coarser elemental and sensory wind-energies. The process of this 'isolation' begins in the second phase and is completed in the third phase of 'isolating the essence of mind'.

The heart-chakra, which is the principal chakra, consists of six knots formed by the two side channels coiling around the Central Channel, three times each. Whereas in all the other chakras the two side-channels coil around the Central Channel only once, each forming a two-fold knot which is relatively easier to untie, at the heart-chakra, the two side channels coil three times each, tightly constricting the Central Channel. From the Central Channel there emanate the eight spokes of the heart-chakra in eight cardinal directions. In the centre of this eight-spoked chakra, within the Central Channel, is contained the 'indestructible drop' composed of the original subtle white and red drops of one's parents, and within this drop is located the Fundamental Innate Mind of Clear Light and its associated wind-energy.

At death, the six-fold knot at the heart-chakra completely unravels and the winds flowing in the side channels enter into the Central Channel and absorb into the indestructible drop located there, whereby all gross levels of consciousness cease and the 'Mother' Clear Light of Death becomes manifest. The meditator of Secret Mantra, who has attained proficiency in unloosening the knot at the navel-chakra, now shifts his attention to unloosening the knots at the heart-chakra. This is accomplished through a special three-step yoga of breath-control (Sanskrit: *Pranayama*) called Vajra Japa (Vajra recitation).

In the first step, one focuses on the indestructible drop at the heart-chakra, visualizing it as a mantric seed-syllable such as HUNG (ཧཱུྃ), focusing specifically on the Nada (squiggle) at the upper tip of the HUNG-syllable. Such intense focusing causes the winds from the upper and lower portion of the body to gather at the heart-chakra, and to partially enter there and dissolve into the indestructible drop. This gives rise to the subtle mind, on the partial dissolution of the grosser minds.

In the second step, the actual 'Pranayama' meditation is done through focusing intensely on a tiny visualized light-drop at the tip of the nose. As one's breath passes by this light-drop, one imagines that the three phases of breathing, i.e. inhalation, pause and exhalation, reverberate as the mantric seed-syllables OM, AH, HUM. These three syllables symbolize the 'Three Vajras' (indestructible realities) of the body, speech and mind of an Enlightened Buddha. In this 'Vajra-recitation', through conjoining one's breath with such intense focusing, the wind-energies are made to enter the Central Channel at the heart-chakra and to move up and down in rhythm with the mantric syllables. This forces the channel-knots to loosen further, allowing the wind-energies to absorb into the indestructible drop, and the first subtle level of mind up to 'white-appearance' arises.

In the third step, the meditator enters into sexual union

with a real or imagined consort, causing the drops to melt and flow down the Central Channel. These drops are then held at the point where one's Central Channel meets the Central Channel of one's consort through the union of the sexual organs. Due to the sustained retention of the drops at that point, the experience of Great Bliss causes the winds to enter more forcefully into the indestructible drop, thereby making the experience of the subtle mind of 'white appearance' more vivid.

When this mind of 'white appearance' has been vividly experienced due to partial loosening of the knots at the heart-chakra through the three steps, the meditator is now ready to move to the third phase of the Completion Stage—the 'isolation of the essence of mind'.

ISOLATING THE ESSENCE OF MIND

> '*Now the indivisible emptiness–luminosity, the naked mind, is stripped bare and dwells in its uncreated state.*'
> —The Bardo Thodrol

During the third phase of the Completion Stage, the meditator completely isolates the 'essence of mind' i.e. the very subtle, constant Clear-Light Mind, from all temporary grosser levels of mind. One meditates on the previously generated image of emptiness with this very subtle mind. In order to accomplish this, the six-fold knot at the heart-chakra must be completely untied so that all the wind-energies coursing throughout the body are actually withdrawn into the Central Channel at the heart-chakra. Such a complete withdrawal and dissolution of all the wind-energies occurs normally only at death.

Though internal yogas such as Chandali Yoga and Vajra

Japa (Vajra-recitation) can bring some of the five root winds into the heart-chakra, it is not possible with these methods alone to gather the 'all-pervading' wind-energy (Sanskrit: *Vyapana*; one of the five root wind-energies) which pervades the whole body and is responsible for movement of all the joints and for tactile sensation. In order to bring about the dissolution of all the five root wind-energies before death, including the 'all-pervading' wind-energy, one must supplement the internal yogas of Chandali and Vajra Japa with sexual union with an actual consort. A celibate yogi can only come up to the point of 'energy-isolation' through using a visualized consort. In order to proceed any further, one must enter into sexual union with a partner of the opposite sex, or must wait for the natural dissolution of all the wind-energies at the point of death in order to actualize the level of 'isolating the essence of mind'.

In general, any person of the opposite sex is not a suitable partner for practising the Tantric yogas. The Tantras specify in detail many qualities and qualifications of such a person. In the Tantras, such a person is referred to as a 'Karma-mudra' because one encounters such a person (or persons) entirely due to one's previous karma. Such karma-mudras are said to be of three types—'field-born', those who are born in one of the sacred 'power-spots' such as the twenty-four sacred points of the mandala of Vajra Yogini which lie in the Indian subcontinent; 'Mantra-born', those partners whom one encounters due to the power of one's mantra (i.e. wind-energy control); and 'spontaneously-born' partners who are emanations of Buddhas and Bodhisattvas meant to specifically assist a particular advanced practitioner of the Completion Stage.

Within these divisions, the consort should be one of the

five types of male and female partners which are specified in classical Indian erotica such as the *Kamasutra*. These classifications are made according to the shape and other qualities of a person's sexual organ, because different types confer and sustain different types and levels of bliss. For instance, among females, the pre-eminent type of consort is said to be of the lotus (Padmini) type. Further, one must be skilled in the famous 'sixty-four arts of love' expounded in the classical treatises on the subject.

To attain Complete Enlightenment as the Three-Bodies of a Buddha while one is alive, one must gather all the wind-energies at the heart-chakra in order to manifest the subtlest level of mind. To do that, one must fully utilize one's sexual faculty of bliss through skilful sexual union.[4] The Tantras say that a lustful person can attain Enlightenment doing what one likes doing the most without following austere ascetic paths, provided one has the intellectual, ethical and physical qualities necessary for a Tantric Warrior. King Indrabodhi, the original recipient of the *Guhyasamaja Tantra*, is an example of such a person. However, many great yogis like Lama Tsongkhapa, who followed the path of complete celibacy, chose to wait for death rather than set a bad example to their celibate monk followers by taking a consort, even though he was fully qualified to do so.

THE ULTIMATE SEMBLANT CLEAR LIGHT

In order to effect the third phase of 'mind-isolation', a qualified yogi would enter into sexual union with an appropriate consort as the 'external' method. Internally, one would ignite the 'inner-fire' of Chandali and/or practise the Vajra-recitation of the second-phase. Holding the vision of oneself and one's partner as the deity and consort, one would emit a flash of light from one's heart-point and dissolve the residence and resident mandalas into light. This light would then absorb into one's body which, in turn, would absorb into the HUNG-syllable at one's heart-point. As the HUNG-syllable dissolves from the bottom upwards, one would experience the eight signs of dissolution until, with practise, all the wind-energies including the 'all-pervading' one would enter, abide and dissolve into the indestructible drop at the heart-point. This would give rise to the final 'Child-Clear Light'. A similar practice was followed during the Generation Stage yogas, but there the dissolution was just imagined, while here the dissolution actually occurs due to the yogi's proficiency in the wind-yogas.

When, through such external and internal methods, all the wind-energies are gathered and dissolved at the heart-point, the 'final' Clear-Light Mind becomes manifest, just as at death. The mind cannot become subtler than this. When this very subtle Clear-Light Mind meditates single-pointedly on an image of emptiness, such a mind is called the Ultimate Semblant Clear Light. It is called 'Ultimate' because all the wind-energies have ceased at the heart-point. It is called 'semblant' because the mind has not yet realized emptiness non-dually, i.e., without the medium of a mentally generated image. Such non-dual cognition of emptiness with the very subtle Clear-Light Mind occurs only in the fourth phase of the Completion Stage, where the subjective Clear-Light Mind and the objective emptiness are undifferentiable.

Thus, when the final Clear-Light Mind arises, and one meditates on an image of emptiness with that mind, the third level of 'isolating the essence of mind' of the Completion Stage is accomplished. Although the cognition of emptiness is still slightly dualistic with a sense of a subject and an object, this is a profound level of attainment. Such a meditator is certain to become Completely Enlightened within that lifetime.

THE SEMBLANT APPARITIONAL BODY

The moment the first experience of this Clear-Light Mind ceases during the meditative session and the wind-energies begin to stir again, instead of arising in one's old body of flesh and blood, the meditator arises in a new subtle body. This is similar to the body of one's meditative deity (Yidam) that one has cultivated throughout the Generation and Completion Stages. This body, though an actual body, is not made of flesh and blood but of the subtle wind-energies. With this body, one can leave one's old body, and experience the subtle level of reality in ways inconceivable to us. This body, similar to the dream-body, can be perceived only by oneself and by those yogis who have secured the same or higher level of attainment.

Inconceivable supernormal powers and clairvoyance are gained with the attainment of this apparitional body. One can leave one's body at will, and can also enter into the dead body of any other person or animal and animate it. One can appear in various animate and inanimate forms, travel anywhere in the universe in an instant and see the past and future lives of oneself and of others. One can also overcome the possibility of untimely, unforeseen death, thus ensuring the attainment of Complete Enlightenment in that very life. Such an apparitional body is also called an 'impure' or 'semblant' apparitional body because it is not yet the actual body of the deity.

One's old body of flesh and blood becomes like a residence for this subtle body which abides in the heart-chakra. One can then move about and appear normally before others who would not notice anything different.

THE ACTUAL CLEAR LIGHT—THE ULTIMATE TRUTH

'O child of noble family, listen. Now the pure luminosity of the dharmata is shining before you, recognize it. O child of noble family, at this moment your state of mind is by nature pure emptiness, it does not possess any nature whatever, neither substance nor quality such as colour, but it is pure emptiness; this is the dharmata, the female Buddha Samantabhadri. But this state of mind is not just blank emptiness, it is unobstructed, sparkling, pure and vibrant; this mind is the male Buddha Samantabhadra. These two, your mind whose nature is emptiness without any substance whatever, and your mind which is vibrant and luminous, are inseparable; this is the Dharmakaya of the Buddha. This mind of yours is inseparable luminosity and emptiness in the form of a great mass of light, it has no birth or death, therefore it is the Buddha of Immortal Light. To recognize this is all that is necessary.'

—The Bardo Thodrol

Having attained the Ultimate Semblant Clear Light and having arisen from that samadhi in the 'impure' semblant apparitional body, the yogi now repeatedly enters into the Clear Light samadhi through using the external method of a karma-mudra, and the internal method of wind dissolution. In one's behaviour, one cultivates the three secret modes of conduct called 'elaborate', 'unelaborate' and 'very unelaborate'; through which the meditator overcomes all dualities of clean and unclean, good and evil, pure and impure. All duality is resolved in the one-taste of bliss-emptiness.

It is said that Naropa, when he reached this level of practice, was found wandering in the streets like a mad man, chanting the Tantric 'code word' 'Vaidurya, Vaidurya'.[5] Someone in the street who understood what it meant, handed Naropa a sharp razor, which Naropa put in his mouth and it melted like butter, with a heavenly taste.

The king, on hearing of the matter, invited Naropa to his residence where he venerated him as a great yogi and offered him one of his daughters. Naropa retreated with his consort outside the limits of the town where they were seen cavorting and openly engaging in orgiastic conduct by many. Fearing that this would corrupt the morals of the people, the elders reported the matter to the king. On verifying the truth of the report, the king had Naropa and his consort thrashed, bound and imprisoned. Naropa pleaded his innocence, stating that he was not at fault and, in order to prove it, he and his consort challenged the king to put them through the test of fire. Accordingly, a sandalwood pyre was made and the couple was placed on it. On being lit, the fire blazed for seven days amidst a dense haze of fragrant smoke. On the seventh day, when the smoke cleared, the couple was found seated in union, radiant with a rainbow light. In a spontaneous song of realization, Naropa sang of how the beating and fire had destroyed the last vestiges of clinging to duality. Padmasambhava is also said to have undergone a similar ordeal by fire in the company of his consort, the princess Mandarava of Zahor.

Through repeated cultivation of the Clear Light Samadhi, focused on a conceptual image of emptiness, the meditator gradually overcomes the dualistic cognition of emptiness. Before attaining direct cognition of emptiness, the meditator receives various signs and omens. On making extensive offerings and prayers to one's guru, the guru appears in the form of the deity and the disciple assumes the semblant apparitional body which is similar to the deity. At midnight, the Guru-Deity confers the third initiation; this time presenting the disciple with a subtle divine consort, who has the form of the deity's consort. On entering into union with that consort, all the wind-energies are completely and forcefully withdrawn into the very subtle wind-energy. The Ultimate Clear-Light Mind becomes manifest. Through focusing it on emptiness, dualistic cognition, via the medium of an image, is completely overcome. The subjective Clear-Light Mind comprehends universal emptiness nakedly, non-dually, where the subjective Clear Light and the Objective Emptiness are undifferentiable. In this way, the meditator attains the Tantric 'Ultimate Truth' which is also called the 'Ultimate-meaning Clear Light' (Sanskrit: *Paramarth-abhaswara*), where the Ultimate Clear-Light Mind is 'sealed' with non-dual cognition of emptiness.

In the sixth and final phase of the Completion Stage, the 'Ultimate-meaning Clear Light' is transformed into the omniscient Dharmakaya of a Buddha. Through directly cognizing emptiness in a non-dual manner with the very subtle Clear-Light Mind, the meditator of Secret Mantra now becomes an 'Arya' (noble) being. Although externally, one may look like a beggar, as in the case of Yogi Mila-Repa, internally, one has joined the most exalted aristocracy—that holy community of beings who have directly realized the true nature of reality and are destined to become 'Universal Emperors', i.e. Buddhas.

THE ACTUAL APPARITIONAL BODY (Sanskrit: *Maya Deha*):—THE CONVENTIONAL TRUTH

The moment the samadhi on the 'Ultimate Meaning Clear Light' ceases and the wind-energy stirs, the meditator achieves the 'Pure' Apparitional Body of the Deity. One also becomes a Secret Mantra 'Arhat' (Foe-Destroyer) because at this stage, the meditator attains liberation (Nirvana) from cyclic existence, having forever destroyed the enemy of ignorance that binds one to compulsive rebirth and death. However, one does not 'fade away', as in the case of the Hinayana Arhat, because one has attained the pure Apparitional Body due to one's strong Bodhichitta aspiration to benefit others.

Although at this stage the meditator overcomes the 'afflictive obstructions' (Sanskrit: *Kleshavarana*) of the delusions, the subtle 'cognitive obstruction' (Sanskrit: *Gyeavarana*) that prevents simultaneous cognition of the Two Truths still remains to be overcome. The meditator cannot as yet retain the Ultimate-Meaning Clear Light while abiding in the Pure Apparitional Body, which are the Two Truths according to Highest Secret Mantra. When the Pure Apparitional Body arises, the Ultimate Clear Light Samadhi ceases and vice versa. This 'final' duality between the Ultimate and Conventional Truths constitutes the actual 'Obstruction to Omniscience'. The resolution of this duality occurs in the final 'Yuganaddha' (assembling together) of the sixth and final phase of the Completion Stage.

With the accomplishment of the Ultimate-Meaning Clear Light and the Pure Apparitional Body, the meditator has effected a complete separation between one's gross body and mind and the subtle mind and its wind-energy. One is now completely free from one's body of flesh and blood. If one wishes, one can leave it, or one can continue to use it in the manner of a Nirmanakaya to benefit and teach others. The meditator has now attained the basis of a Buddha's omniscient Dharmakaya and omnipresent Rupakaya. One does not have to attain new paths; now the formless Clear Light and Pure Apparitional Form have to be 'assembled' together.

YUGANADDHA—THE FINAL UNION OF THE TWO TRUTHS

Since no new paths have to be followed, the meditator practises immersing the Pure Apparitional Body into the Ultimate-Meaning Clear Light through the external yoga of union with the divine consort, and the internal yoga of dissolving the divine world (mandala) into light, and then absorbing that light inwards into the heart-point. In the post-meditation period, the meditator continues to engage in the three types of 'elaborate', 'unelaborate' and 'very unelaborate' conduct. The purpose is to reduce the 'distance' between formless meditative equipoise on the Ultimate-Meaning Clear Light and action with the Pure Apparitional Body so that the two are blended to the point where there is no separation between 'meditation' and 'post-meditation'.

The Tantras say that in about six months after having attained the Pure Apparitional Form, the yogi will approach the point of Enlightenment. At midnight, the guru and all the Buddhas will actually manifest in the pure Sambhogakaya form of the Meditation Deity (Yidam) and will confer the Third Empowerment of Transcendent Wisdom. At that time, in the pure apparitional body, the meditator will unite with the actual divine consort of the Yidam Deity. Due to this, all grosser-levels of the dualistic mind absorb and cease forever, never to manifest again.

The practitioner remains in this meditative equipoise

till dawn during which time the very subtle Obstructions to Omniscience (Sanskrit: *Gye-avarana*) are overcome completely and forever. At dawn, when the sky is free of darkness, moonlight and sunlight, one attains Complete Omniscience, and one's Pure Apparitional Body becomes the Sambhogakaya of a fully Enlightened Buddha.

This state is described in terms of seven distinctive characteristics:

1. Perfect form: One's body of light is adorned with the thirty-two major and eighty minor marks of physical perfection such as the crown protrusion (*Ushnisha*), curling hair at the brow-point (*Urna*), elongated ears and perfect body proportions.
2. Perfect enjoyment: One is in the constant embrace of a perfect consort, resident in a perfect mandala, with a perfect retinue. All pure sensory objects are constantly and rapturously enjoyed.
3. Perfect bliss: One's mind abides in a constant, unfluctuating state of Great Bliss.
4. Perfect cognition: This constant mind of Great Bliss is indivisible from universal emptiness, in which all phenomena of Samsara and Nirvana are simultaneously cognized in the 'vast equilibrium of reality'.
5. Perfect compassion: While seeing the illusory nature of all beings and their sufferings, the mind is constantly suffused with undiminishing compassion for each being, good and evil, in all the inconceivable worlds—from hell to the peak of cyclic existence. Untainted by even the slightest trace of selfish concern, one is constantly mindful of the benefit of all beings.
6. Immortality: The continuum of one's perfect form,

which is impermanent as it changes from instant to instant, is permanent in the sense that its type does not alter, and it undergoes no birth, ageing, sickness or death.

7. Perfect Enlightened Activity: While one's Body of Perfect Rapture remains 'inwardly radiant' in a constant and undiminishing manner, one's physical emanations (Nirmanakayas) pervade everywhere in the Trifold Chilliocosm[6] as its 'outward' radiance. In this way, one appears as 'supreme Nirmanakayas', like Shakyamuni Buddha, for beings who have the karma to perceive one in that form; one appears as a guru, spiritual friend, teacher, leader, artisan or poet. One can manifest even as inanimate objects like oases in deserts, bridges over chasms, food and medicine, in order to benefit beings according to their karma. Such enlightened activity is ceaseless and completely effortless, performed without moving from one's own timeless, Ultimate Clear Light Samadhi, which transcends space, time and all duality. The attainment of the Dharmakaya and the Rupakaya is simultaneous, the former being one's own ultimate benefit, while the latter is the ultimate benefit of others.

One's old body of flesh and blood remains[7] as a shell, a Nirmanakaya, which is now animated by one's 'inwardly radiant' Sambhogakaya, whose mind is the omniscient Dharmakaya. As this Completely Enlightened 'triple-being', one attains union with the perfect body, speech and mind of one's guru—the goal of Guru Yoga. Through manifesting the Nirmanakaya, one also completely fulfils one's Bodhisattva vow to work ceaselessly for the benefit of all sentient beings. Since beings are infinite in number, it will take an eternity of time to accomplish this. Thus, as His

Holiness the Dalai Lama often says, quoting the Bodhisattva Shantideva—

> 'For as long as space exists,
> For as long as living beings remain,
> Until then may I too abide
> To dispel the misery of the world.'

Conclusion

THE THREE CRUCIAL problems that any genuine spiritual warrior must resolve are those of: death, anger-sexuality, and the true nature of reality. With death always just a breath away in this increasingly polluted, violent and turbulent world, the spiritual warrior must be in readiness whenever and in whatever manner death may arrive. Secondly, one's anger and sexuality can be a problem even graver than death, specially for spiritual warriors who are by nature passionate people. And thirdly, the all-encompassing problem of what exactly is the true nature of reality—the problem of individual and universal purpose. Quite clearly there are no political or economic or social solutions to these problems.

The Buddhist path of Highest Secret Mantra directly addresses these three problems in a precise and final manner. It shows the warrior how to harness the energy of sexuality and wrath, which, if left unharnessed, can actually be dangerous and destructive; and how to use this energy to resolve the problems of death and the true nature of reality. In resolving these crucial problems, one not only benefits oneself but is also of use to others.

Also, just as mere knowledge of a remedy is not sufficient to actually cure an illness—one must take the medicine and follow the required regimen—similarly, mere intellectual knowledge of this profound path is not enough. One must actually practise and accomplish each step, overlooking nothing. In one's search for, and in the practise of, a true spiritual path, one should be mindful of the Buddha's advice concerning the 'Four Reliances'. First, while searching for a true guru, one should not be swayed by such superficial aspects as the teacher's fame, status, wealth, titles; rather one should examine the teachings of a guru, and whether or not they make sense. Secondly, while examining the teachings of a guru, one should not get carried away by impressive, high-sounding words and rhetoric, but should rely on the meaning of what is taught. Thirdly, while observing the meaning, one should not rely on teachings concerning mundane aspects of reality such as politics, poetry, medicine and astrology; one should rather rely on the definitive meaning concerning the ultimate nature of reality, i.e. the profound emptiness. Fourthly, one should not be satisfied with a mere intellectual comprehension of it, but should seek direct, non-dual experience.

The wind-energy yogas of the channels, chakras and drops are also found in certain non-Buddhist Tantric traditions prevalent in India in ancient and contemporary times. What distinguishes the Buddhist systems from the non-Buddhist ones is the profound doctrine of Emptiness and the supreme compassionate Bodhichitta motivation of universal responsibility. The whole orientation of the Buddhist path of Highest Secret Mantra is focused on the realization of the profound universal Emptiness with the very Subtle Clear-Light Mind so that one may fulfil one's

Bodhisattva vow by manifesting the omnipresent Rupakaya, for the ceaseless benefit of others. Without such a correct view of Emptiness and without the universal Bodhichitta motivation, it may be possible to practise the yogas of the winds, channels and drops, but this would, at the most, lead to the attainment of some mundane siddhis (magical powers) and/or to rebirth in the sensory heavens of the Desire Realm.

It is said that a Tibetan yogi who practised the Generation Stage of the Highest Secret Mantra Deity, Vajra Bhairava Yamantaka (a very wrathful deity who has the head of a ferocious bull), was reborn as a bull-headed demon, because he lacked the correct view and motivation. Without the correct view of Emptiness, it would be impossible to practise the Deity Yoga of the Generation Stage because that yoga is wholly based on a union of Bliss and Emptiness. Furthermore, it would not be possible to attain the ultimate-meaning Clear Light (Sanskrit: *Paramarthabhasvara*) which is a non-dual fusion of the subjective Clear Light Consciousness and universal Emptiness. Also, it would be impossible to reach the supreme attainment of the Rupakaya because its attainment is solely based on the Ultimate Meaning Clear Light and the Bodhichitta vow. In other words, it would be impossible to gain Buddhahood outside the tradition of Buddhist Highest Secret Mantra.

His Holiness the Dalai Lama once admonished me, saying that even if I attained the ability to fly through the yogas of the wind-energies, channels and drops, it would be no great achievement, as the essence of the path is Bodhichitta. And the basis of Bodhichitta is taking refuge in the Three Precious Jewels—the Buddha, the Dharma and the Sangha—and living one's life accordingly.

In conclusion, I accept complete responsibility for any errors that may have crept into the narrative, and beg for the indulgence of the Gurus, Yidams and Protectors of the tradition of Highest Secret Mantra. Any merit that may accrue from the composition and writing of this book is wholly dedicated to the Complete Enlightenment of all mother sentient beings.

Dharmaraja Yama and consort Chamundi Devi

Appendix-I

TANTRIC VIEW OF THE HISTORICAL BUDDHA

ACCORDING TO THE scriptures of the Hinayana school, the Buddha Shakyamuni was born as the prince of the Shakya clan, in his last rebirth as an ordinary individual. Having accumulated vast merit (*punya*) in past lives, he completed the path in that last lifetime. Then, seated under the Bodhi Tree at Vajrasana in Magadha, he attained Complete Enlightenment (*Samma Sambodhi*) and became a Buddha. Having established the holy Sangha community, he extensively 'turned the wheel of Dharma' for this world-age. He then passed away into 'Pari-nirvana'—a cessation without remainder.

According to the tradition of Highest Secret Mantra, Buddha Shakyamuni did not attain Enlightenment under the Bodhi tree, he merely made manifest the Enlightened state, which he had already attained many aeons earlier in the Akanishta Paradise, in the Realm of Pure Form. The Buddha first practised the Mahayana path of the Six Perfections (*Paramitas*) for three 'Great Aeons' of time. Having attained the Tenth Bodhisattva level (*Bhumi*) at the end of that period, he was reborn as a god in the Akanishta Paradise of Pure Form, whose body is ornamented with the thirty-two major and eighty minor signs of physical perfection.

Having attained direct cognition of Emptiness on the Bodhisattva path, he abided in meditative equipoise on Emptiness. He was aroused from this by the Sambhogakaya of the Buddhas of the past who instructed him in the Path of Highest Secret Mantra by pointing out to him that it was impossible to attain the omniscient mind and omnipresent form of a Buddha without actualizing the Ultimate-Meaning Clear Light (Sanskrit: *Paramarthabhasvara*). As he had already attained the perfect form of a deity and Brahma-like speech, he did not require the first and second initiations of Highest Secret Mantra (the Vase and Secret Empowerments). Accordingly, he received the third Transcendent-Wisdom Empowerment, during which he was presented with the divine consort, Devi Tilottama.

On uniting with her, the Buddha was able to withdraw all the wind-energies into the very subtle wind-energy at the heart-point. On experiencing the Ultimate Clear-Light Mind, he was able to non-dually cognize Universal Emptiness with that mind, thereby attaining the Ultimate-meaning Clear Light. Arising from that samadhi in a Pure Apparitional Body, he re-entered the Clear Light Samadhi and attained the Yuganaddha-Union of the Two Truths, and became a Completely Enlightened Buddha.

Eventually, when the karma and merit of the beings of this world matured, he manifested as the Supreme Nirmanakaya, as prophesied by previous Buddhas. As with all the Supreme Nirmanakayas, his physical body was ornamented with the major and minor signs of perfection, and he performed the twelve main deeds[1] of a Supreme Nirmanakaya which appears to 'turn the wheel of Dharma' for a particular world-age.

The Supreme Nirmanakayas of 1,000 Buddhas will appear during this great world-age (Maha-kalpa), whereby it is called the 'Bhadra-kalpa' (fortunate world-age), as there are world-ages where no Supreme Nirmanakayas appear due to the lack of merit of beings. Buddha Shakyamuni was the fourth Supreme Nirmanakaya. The next prophesied Supreme Nirmanakaya will be that of the Buddha Maitreya, who will appear four billion nine hundred million human years from now. The 'dharma-reign' (Buddha Shasana) of the present Buddha Shakyamuni will last for a total of 5,000 human years, of which about 2,500 have already passed.

Appendix-II

BUDDHIST/TANTRIC COSMOLOGY

WHEN REALITY IS perceived through the eyes of a fully enlightened Buddha, unclouded by even the slightest trace of ignorance or imperfection, it appears as the perfect mandala of the Three Kayas. When viewed through the 'ordinary' eyes of sentient beings, clouded by many layers of innate and acquired ignorance, reality variously appears in accordance with their individual and collective karma, as the three realms of cyclic existence—*samsara*. The Dharmakaya appears as the 'Formless Realm' (Sanskrit: *Arupa-lok*), accessible only to formless meditators; the Sambhogakaya appears as the 'Realm of Pure Form' (Sanskrit: *Rupalok*), accessible to meditators on pure forms; and the Nirmanakaya appears as the 'Desire Realm' (Sanskrit: *Kama-lok*), where the vast majority of sentient beings exist, from the Sensory Paradises of the Desire Realm down to animals, ghosts and beings from hell.

The gross universe of matter, space, time and energy, which is the object of the scientific materialist paradigm, is perceived only by beings of the Desire Realm, and not by those of the higher realms who perceive (and act in) reality at increasingly subtle levels. Within the view of the material universe as it appears to humans, the Buddhist view is of a Cyclic Material Universe—where world-systems form, abide, disintegrate and re-form again in a beginningless and endless cosmic cycle that spans eternity. The characteristics and experiences of each formation and disintegration are entirely dependent on the collective karma of all sentient beings from a previous world-age (Kalpa). Each Mahakalpa (great aeon) consists of twenty intermediate aeons each for formation, abiding, disintegration, and vacuity, totalling eighty intermediate aeons. One great aeon of time consists of ten, followed by fifty-nine zeros (10^{59}) number of human years.

At the beginning of a world-age, space forms from very subtle 'space-particles' that arise from the vacuity due to the collective karma of beings from the previous world-age. Due to the aggregation of these space-particles, a semi-circular 'blue wind' begins stirring, forming the gaseous 'wind' element from space. Due to the movement of this wind, there arises incandescent heat in the form of a red triangle of the fire element. Due to the combined action of these three elements, seven types of 'precious substances' condense to form the vast ocean in the form of a white circle of the water element, supported by dense winds, with the primordial fire in its depths. From the combined action of these arises the solid earth-element in the form of a golden square. This subdivides to form the central axis of Mount Sumeru, surrounded by four major continents and eight subcontinents.

At the end of the previous world-age, when the world-system of the desire realm was gradually destroyed during the twenty aeons of disintegration, sentient beings were spontaneously reborn in lower paradises of the realm of Pure Form. Then, after twenty aeons of vacuity, when the world systems began to re-form, these sentient beings were again drawn to the material worlds that were forming, due to attachment and previous karma. After the formation of the Desire-Realm heavens, our own world began to re-form in the manner described above, and the beings of this world arrived here. In the beginning, their bodies were made of subtle luminous matter, they could fly in the air and needed no material food, deriving their energy from the subtle bliss of natural meditative absorption (samadhi). At that time, sexual differentiation had not arisen and all had similar sexless bodies and minds.

Then, gradually, the earth's surface became covered by a nutrient substance, which these beings were drawn into eating because of their previous karma. Due to consuming this nutrient, their bodies lost their luminosity; they became earth-bound and sexual organs appeared. As sexual differentiation began, dwellings were built to conceal the sexual act, and the convention of physical death and rebirth through the womb became established.

At that time, the beings were naturally virtuous and therefore enjoyed excellent health, good physical stature and exceedingly long lives. Food grew all over the earth and did not need to be cultivated through effort. But as dwellings and communities were established, due to greed, food, goods, and mates were hoarded in excess of need, depriving others. Due to this, some began stealing and killing. In this way, the cycle of non-virtuous negative karma began and the conditions for rebirth in the three 'lower realms' of animals, ghosts, and hells came into existence. The twenty aeons of formation of the 'Trifold Chilliocosm' (Sanskrit: *Tri-sahasrara-Maha-sahasrara-loka-dhatu*) of this world-age was finished when a thousand times thousand times thousand such worlds were completed with the worlds of gods, demigods, humans, animals, ghosts and beings from hell, providing suitable birthplaces for beings in accordance with their karmic dispositions.

During the twenty aeons of abiding of the world system, the lifespan and fortune of beings fluctuate and undergo several cycles in accordance with their collective karma. Presently, we, of the 'Degenerate Era' (Kali Yuga), are on a decline. As concepts, ideas and objects proliferate, the causes of non-virtue increase and the collective negative karma of beings increases correspondingly. The average lifespan of beings decreases, environments degenerate, food has to be procured with greater and greater hardship, and delusions such as greed and anger are all powerful. Eventually, the average lifespan of beings will become a mere fifteen years, everyone will carry weapons, and there will be large-scale destruction due to natural calamities, war, famine and disease. Then, the emanation-bodies (Nirmanakayas) of Buddhas and Bodhisattvas will appear to guide beings on the path of virtue. As a result, the fortune and lifespan of beings will again begin to increase. When the next decline begins, the Supreme Nirmanakaya of the Buddha Maitreya will appear in our world to again turn the Wheel of Dharma for that world-age.

When a thousand such Supreme Emanation Bodies have appeared, during many cycles of increase and decline, this Great World Age (Mahakalpa) will end and the world-system will undergo destruction. All the remaining beings (the majority), who have not attained liberation or

Enlightenment, will be spontaneously reborn in the higher Realms of Paradise. After twenty aeons of vacuity, the cycle will start all over again. In this, there will be no Creator or Created apart from an unsubdued mind.

Notes

Introduction

1. Swaraswati and Manju Ghosh are, respectively, the female and male Buddhist deities of learning and wisdom. They are traditionally invoked at the commencement of a text such as this.

2-3. All technical terms are explained at length in later chapters and in the Glossary.

4. Vajradhara Guru is explained at length in chapter 4.

5. For Geluk-pa order, see chapter 1 on Tantric History.

6. Highest Yoga Tantra is explained extensively in the course of the text.

7. Lam-Rim is the 'gradual sequence' of the path to Enlightenment followed by the Geluk-pa order.

Tantric History

1. Synonyms: Tantrayana, (guhya) Mantrayana, path of Secret Mantra.

2. For details of their lives, see Taranatha's *Blue Annals*, translated by George Roerich et al, published by Motilal Banarsidas. Also, *Buddha's Lions* by Tarthang Tulku et al, Dharma Publishing, Berkeley, US.

3. Rainbow Body is the body of light that arises at the culmination of the Completion Stage of Highest Secret Mantra.

4. Yakshinis are supernatural beings belonging to the class of demigods.

5. His Holiness, Gyalwa Tenzin Gyatso, the present Dalai Lama, was born in a peasant family from Amdo in north-eastern Tibet. For details of the finding of his present incarnation, see *Kalachakra Tantra* by His Holiness the Dalai Lama, translated by Jeffry Hopkins, Wisdom Publications.

The Tantric Practitioner

1. Note that the word 'self' has two different meanings in the two terms 'self-grasping' and 'self-cherishing'. In the former, it means 'absolute existence' and in the latter, it refers to the sense of ego, or 'I' that we feel all the time. The latter being the effect of the former.

2. 'Five Great Logical Devices' of the Madhyamikas are:
1. Dependent-existence: that establishes all phenomena as being empty because of being dependent-existents.
2. Diamond points: that refute absolute production.
3. Seven-point analysis: that refute absolute systems through refuting 'sameness' and 'difference' of the designated object and its basis of designation.
4. Four extremes: that refute absolute production.
5. Four alternatives: that refute the absolute existence of causes and effects.

Tantric World View

1. To be explained in the following chapter.

2. When the Sambhogakaya and the Nirmanakaya are together subsumed under the single category of 'Form' or 'Form Body' (Sanskrit: *Rupakaya*), the Three Bodies can also be spoken of as Two-Bodies—the formless Dharmakaya and the form of the Rupakaya.

The Tantric Guru

1. Translated in English with a commentary by Geshe Ngawang-Dhargyey, published by the Library of Tibetan Works and Archives, Dharamsala, 1975.

2.If one has received the Four Initiations of Highest Secret Mantra, then prior to the visualization, one visualizes the Guru-Deity in front and receives the Four Initiations in the form of lights from the Guru-Deity's three points of body, speech and mind.

3. The objects of the five senses are included within the category of 'Form'.

4. For details of 'Thirty-Five Confession Buddhas', see *The Preliminary Practices of Tibetan Buddhism* by Geshe Rapten, published by the Library of Tibetan Works and Archives, Dharamsala.

5. Kusha grass is the grass used by the Buddha for his seat under the Bodhi tree.

6. In some descriptions of this mandala, Vairochana and consort are in the centre, and Akshobhya and consort are in the east.

The Tantric Path

1. The four demons that afflict and thwart the practitioner on the path—(1) Deva-Putra Mara: the demon of desire; (2) Klesha-Mara: the demon of delusions; (3) Skandha-Mara: the demon of the contaminated psychophysical aggregates; (4) Mrityu-Mara: the demon of untimely death.

2. See Appendix-II.

3. According to the Tantric view even females emit regenerative fluid during orgasm, although in not as obvious and copious a manner as a male.

4. For a Tantric view of the Enlightenment of the Buddha Shakyamuni, see Appendix-I.

5. A blue precious stone, probably beryl, which has medicinal properties.

6. See Appendix-II.

7. In the Kalachakra Tantric system, one's body of flesh and blood, said to be composed of 21,600 impure karmic wind-energies, is gradually dematerialized into light by the experience of 21,600 'Immutable Blisses', until one attains the 'Pure Empty Form' of the Deity Kalachakra.

Appendix I

1. Twelve main deeds of a Supreme Nirmanakaya: (1) abiding in the Tushita Paradise; (2) descent into the womb; (3) taking birth; (4) education; (5) enjoying sensual pleasure; (6) renouncing the world; (7) practising and rejecting asceticism; (8) reaching the seat of enlightenment at

Bodhgaya; (9) defeating the forces of Mara; (10) manifesting Perfect Enlightenment; (11) turning the wheel of Dharma; (12) passing away into Parinirvana.

Glossary

Adi Buddha: The primordial continuum of Enlightened mind represented by the Old Translation Schools as Buddha Samantabhadra, and by the New Translation Schools as the Buddha Vajradhara.

Akanishta: The highest paradise of the Realm of Form, and the field of activity of the Sambhogakaya.

Anatma: Self-less, synonymous with the profound Emptiness—the core philosophy of Buddhism.

Anitya: Impermanent, momentary, ephemeral—the nature of all composite phenomena.

Atma: Self—the object of negation in the view of selflessness, i.e. Emptiness. For the lower Hinayana philosophical schools it means a permanent, substantially existent person able to exist independently of the five aggregates. For the Prasangika Madhyamika school, 'self' means 'Absolute Existence' (Sanskrit: *Svabhavasiddha*).

Arhat: Foe-destroyer, i.e. someone who has destroyed the enemy of cyclic existence (samsara) and attained liberation.

Arya: Noble, i.e. someone who has attained direct cognition of Emptiness and therefore surpasses all other beings in samsara, including the gods of the higher realms.

Avalokiteshwara: The embodiment of the compassion of all the Buddhas. The patron deity and protector of Tibet, present in the person of the Dalai Lamas.

Avidya: Ignorance—the root cause that binds beings in cyclic existence.

Bindu: The 'white and red drops' that are derived from the sperm and ovum of one's parents, and are responsible for various functions in the physical and subtle bodies.

Bodhichitta: The supreme aspiration to attain Complete Enlightenment for the sake of all other beings. The entry into the Mahayana and Vajrayana paths.

Bodhisattva: Any person who has entered the Mahayana by generating the supreme altruistic aspiration to Complete Enlightenment.

Bon: The pre-Buddhist, native shamanism of Tibet.

Consciousness Transference (Tibetan: *Pho-wa*): One of the Six Yogas of Naropa in which the meditator is able to consciously 'transfer' one's consciousness to a suitable rebirth in a 'Pure land' at the point of one's death.

Chakra: The 'Channel-Wheels' or energy nexus in the subtle energy-body.

Chandali: The 'foundation Yoga' of the Six Yogas of Naropa, dealing with the red-drop located in the navel-chakra.

Dakini: Female yoginis who assist the yogi on the Tantric path. Can be both supernatural beings and women of flesh and blood.

Dharmadhatu: The fundamental expanse of Emptiness which contains all phenomena.

Dharmakaya: The 'Body of Reality'—the omniscient, all pervasive mind of a Buddha.

Dukkha: Suffering—the condition of all unenlightened beings who suffer from the three levels of suffering—the suffering of misery, the suffering of impermanence, and the suffering of the contaminated aggregates.

Dzokchen: Ati-Yoga—the highest level of yoga according to the Old Translation Schools.

Guhyasamaja Tantra: The Fundamental Father Tantra in which the doctrine of the illusory body is expounded in detail.

Hevajra Tantra: The Fundamental Mother Tantra in which the doctrine of Chandali Yoga is expounded in detail.

Heruka Tantra: The Mahasukha Chakrasamvara Tantra—a fundamental Mother Tantra in which the doctrine of the Karma mudra is expounded in detail.

Illusory Body: The mental body generated through the Yogas of the Completion Stage which is the precursor and cause of the immortal, omnipresent Rupakaya of the resultant state of Buddha hood.

Kala Chakra Tantra: The 'Wheel of Time' Tantra—a non-dual Tantra, also sometimes classified as a Mother Tantra, in which the doctrine of Supreme Immutable Bliss and Pure Empty Form are expounded in detail.

Karma: Action through body, speech and mind and its effect on one's future. Specifically, the doctrine of cause and effect, where each life of every being is the effect of former lives and the cause of future lives.

Karma mudra: The sexual partner of the opposite sex who is the 'support of bliss' in the Generation and Completion Stage Yogas.

Lama: Tibetan equivalent of the Sanskrit term 'Guru' meaning 'highest'.

Lo-Jong: The 'mind-transformation' techniques designed to overcome the innate poisons of self-grasping and self-cherishing, taught in Tibet principally by the Indian Guru Dipankara Shri-

Gyan Atisha. An essential prerequisite for Tantric practice.

Mandala: A word with many meanings. In the Tantric context, it refers specifically to the 'Resident' mandala of the Tantric deity and retinue, and the 'Residence' mandala which is the divine abode of the 'Resident' mandala. In general, it means 'system'.

Madhyamika Avatara: 'Entry to the Middle Way'—the fundamental text of the Prasangika Madhyamika system, written by Acharya Chandrakirti.

Maha-anuttara Yoga Tantra: 'Great Unsurpassed Yoga Tantra'—the Highest level of Tantric practice involving the Generation and Completion stages. Synonyms: Vajrayana, Guhya Mantra, Mantrayana, Highest Secret Mantra.

Mahakala: 'The Great Black One'—a wrathful Tantric manifestation of Arya Avalokiteshwara.

Mahasiddha: 'Great Adept'—a term used for the ancient Tantric masters of India.

Mahayana: 'The Great Vehicle' of Buddhism as distinct from the Hinayana, the 'Lesser Vehicle'. The Vajrayana or Tantric vehicle is a part of the Mahayana. Synonyms: Paramitayana, Sutrayana.

Manju Ghosha: Manjushree—'The Melodious Voiced One'—the embodiment of the speech and wisdom of all the Buddhas—the patron deity of the Doctrine of Emptiness and of eloquence.

Mantra: Coded incantations that symbolize various facets of the Enlightened state.

Mudra: Another word with many meanings. Can refer to symbolic hand gestures that are used in ritual, or to the bone ornaments worn by Tantric Deities. Also refers to the consort of the yogi.

Naga: Non-human, serpentine beings with supernatural powers.

Nirmanakaya: 'The body of development'—the physical bodies of Buddhas and Gurus that appear in the human (and other) worlds, in order to guide and teach the Dharma to sentient beings.

Nirvana: The cessation of suffering. Liberation from cyclic existence. The basic aim of all Buddhist practice.

Paramarthasatya: Ultimate Truth. According to the Sutrayana it refers to the Emptiness of all phenomena. According to Highest Secret Mantra it refers to the Ultimate-meaning Clear Light Mind that realizes universal emptiness non-dually.

Paramarth-Abhaswara:The Ultimate-meaning Clear Light Mind which realizes Emptiness non-dually.

Pragya: Transcendent wisdom. The wisdom of Emptiness.

Pragya-paramita Sutras: The teachings of the Buddha which constitute the 'Second Turning of the Wheel of Dharma'. In them, the Buddha has taught the doctrine of Emptiness explicitly and at great length. These Sutras are considered definitive by the Madhyamika system.

Pratitya-Samutpada: Dependent-arising/existence. The philosophical core-doctrine of Buddhism—the positive aspect of Emptiness.

Preta: Ghosts.

Punya: Meritorious karma, which must be accumulated by the Bodhisattva along with Pragya (transcendent wisdom) in order to attain Complete Enlightenment.

Rakshasa: Cannibalistic demonic beings.

Rainbow Body: The body of light that is the precursor of the Rupakaya, attained at the end of the Completion Stage. The meditator who has attained it can vanish in a flash of light.

Rudra: A malign god of the Desire Realm.

Rupakaya: The 'Form Body'—the basic aim of the Tantric

Bodhisattva. It is the immortal, omnipresent form of a Buddha that manifests as the fundamental Sambhogakaya mandala of the Five Tathagatas. It further manifests as the numerous Tantric mandalas and as the Nirmanakayas that appear in all the worlds of cyclic existence.

Sadhana: The meditative visualizations, mantra recitations and rituals pertaining to each Tantric deity.

Sadhu: An Indian mendicant. Holy man.

Samadhi: Meditative equipoise on a subtle internal mental object so that all sensory and other distractions to the 'outside' are eliminated.

Sambhogakaya: 'The Body of Perfect Rapture'—the subtle male-female form of subtle energy that is the actual body of a Buddha, which then appears variously to different trainees in accordance with their karma.

Samvriti Satya: 'Conventional Truth' as distinct from 'Ultimate Truth'. In Sutra, it refers to all phenomena which are the basis of emptiness. In Tantra, it refers to the 'illusory body' as distinct from the formless Ultimate-meaning Clear Light Mind.

Shunyata: Emptiness. The final, actual mode of existence of all phenomena. The Ultimate Truth.

Swabhava Siddha: Absolute Existence. The Object of Negation in the correct view of Emptiness.

Swaraswati: The Indian goddess of learning, melody, and eloquence. The Transcendent Tantric Consort of the Buddha Manjushree.

Sutra: A text containing the actual words of the Buddha on non-Tantric topics.

Sutrayana: 'The Vehicle of the Sutras'—the exoteric canon of Buddhism, incorporating the Hinayana and Mahayana, as distinct from the esoteric Vajrayana or Tantric Vehicle.

Tara: 'The Saviouress'—a female Buddha much loved and revered by Mahayana and Vajrayana Buddhists.

Tathagata Garbha: The 'Buddha Nature' that is the innate nature of all beings, which makes possible the attainment of Buddhahood. According to Sutra, it refers to the Emptiness of the mind, and according to Tantra, it refers to the Fundamental Innate Mind of Clear-Light and its associated wind-energy located in the heart-chakra of all sentient beings.

Trikaya: The 'Three Bodies' of a Fully Enlightened Buddha—the Dharmakaya, the Sambhogakaya and the Nirmanakaya.

Tummo: Tibetan name for Chandali Yoga.

Vajra: A symbolic Tantric hand implement, symbolizing the indestructible reality of enlightened mind. It also symbolizes the male 'Skilful means' as distinct from the female 'Wisdom of Emptiness'—symbolized by a bell.

Vajra Bhairava: 'Indestructible Terrifier', a wrathful deity of Highest Secret Mantra.

Vajra Kilaya: 'Indestructible Nail', a wrathful deity of Highest Secret Mantra, particularly practised by the Old Translation Schools.

Vajra Varahi: 'Indestructible Sow', a semi-wrathful female deity of Highest Secret Mantra. The consort of Heruka Chakrasamvara.

Vajrayana: The Tantric path, synonymous with Mantrayana/Guhyamantrayana.

◙